ACCORDING TO THE SCRIPTURES

According to the Scriptures

*The Origins of the Gospel and
of the Church's Old Testament*

Paul M. van Buren

WILLIAM B. EERDMANS PUBLISHING COMPANY
GRAND RAPIDS, MICHIGAN / CAMBRIDGE, U.K.

© 1998 Wm. B. Eerdmans Publishing Co.
255 Jefferson Ave. S.E., Grand Rapids, Michigan 49503 /
P.O. Box 163, Cambridge CB3 9PU U.K.

Printed in the United States of America

03 02 01 00 99 98   7 6 5 4 3 2 1

Library of Congress Cataloging-in-Publication Data

Van Buren, Paul Matthews, 1924-
  According to the scriptures : the origins of the gospel and of the church's
Old Testament / Paul M. van Buren.
    p.   cm.
  Includes bibliographical references and index.
  ISBN 0-8028-4535-5 (pbk. : alk. paper)
  1. Bible. N.T. Corinthians, 1st, XV, 3-5 — Criticism, interpretation, etc.
2. Bible. O.T. — Criticism, interpretation, etc. — History — Early church,
ca. 30-600. 3. Christianity and other religions — Judaism. 4. Judaism —
Relations — Christianity. 5. Christianity — Origin. I. Title.
BS2675.2.V26   1998
220.6′7 — dc21   98-28327
                                        CIP

Contents

Preface

IN THIS STUDY I am concerned with tracing the origins of the gospel that Paul received, preached, and rehearsed in 1 Corinthians 15:3-5, "that Christ died for our sins in accordance with the scriptures, that he was buried, that he was raised on the third day in accordance with the scriptures, and that he appeared to Cephas, then to the twelve." I began this work with the hope of throwing light on a current problem. There is a growing gap, unsettling for some Christians, between the various pictures of Jesus being drawn by a number of New Testament scholars, and what the church, judging by its Eucharist and creeds, has seemed from very early on to have regarded as Jesus' primary importance. This is, of course, only the contemporary form of the long-standing problem of the Jesus of history and the Christ of faith, made sharper by explorations into the Jewishness of Jesus and such attention-getters as the so-called Jesus Seminar, and by our generally broader and deeper knowledge of Jewish life and thought in the first century of the Common Era. My interest in the subject was also fed by a hope that a better understanding of the origins of the Christian movement might help us understand why the movement later separated itself from the rest of the Jewish people with the degree of hostility already evident in the passion narratives of the Gospels. As the study developed, however, I found that there were serious questions for the church not only about the gospel formulated in accordance with the scriptures, but also about those scriptures in accordance with which the early gospel was formed. Hence the two-part division of the book.

The title I have given this study was dictated by its subject, despite the fact that it was used by the New Testament scholar C. H. Dodd some forty-five years ago for an influential study of a related, but rather different, sort. The task Dodd set himself was to examine how the Old Testament was used to elucidate the *kerygma,* the earliest Christian proclamation about Jesus. Dodd presupposed that the proclamation of the early message, which included the gospel of 1 Corinthians 15:3-5, already existed, and that the apostles then turned to the "Old Testament," which he did not distinguish from the Bible of the Jewish people, to "elucidate" the early message. These presuppositions are no longer possible today. The present study will argue that the Old Testament was constituted by an interpretation of the scriptures of ancient Israel, as these were being read by some Jews of the first century, and that the gospel was the fruit of this same interpretation. The discovery of the gospel and the invention of the Old Testament were both the result of a new reading of Israel's scriptures and so were a single event, two sides of the same coin.

The results of this study both surprised and pleased me. The first was the discovery of how deeply rooted in the Jewish tradition is the central story or myth of the church, formulated in the gospel of the death and resurrection of Jesus. The second was the evidence for the indispensable role of the Old Testament in the formulation of the early gospel, which argues that it could and should be used in the church to identify and correct anti-Judaic polemics in the New Testament.

This study may also help to weaken a number of popular but false ideas. One is that Paul was the inventor of Christianity (this is certainly not to say that Jesus was!). Others are: that a great gulf exists between the Old Testament and the New Testament, that the early Christians used the Old Testament to prove or support their already established belief in Jesus, and that Christianity is less credible or of less value if it is shown to be dependent on Jewish traditions.

In the course of this study, I have had the pleasure of learning from many biblical scholars, as the notes will attest. Two of them are due additional thanks: Donald Juel, of Princeton Theological Seminary, for reading an earlier version of this study and for his encouragement; and Moshe Greenberg, of Hebrew University, for an encouraging response to an earlier version of Chapter 8. The substance of Chapters 3 and 4 has been presented in lectures at the Universities of Basel and Heidelberg and published in *Kirche und Israel* 96 (1996). I wish to thank both Ariane and Anne van Buren for much appreciated editorial assistance, which has helped make this study more readable.

PART I

THE GOSPEL
OF THE SCRIPTURES

Introduction

FROM THE SPRING of about the year 30 C.E. and through the following year, a small group of Jews formed what we may call a Jewish sect. Paul of Tarsus joined the movement toward the end of that brief period, or a year or two later,[1] but the sect was already growing rapidly, evidently in a number of locations, and developing into what we know as the Christian church. Central for an important number among them, presumably from the beginning, was what they called their gospel,[2] the particular story that they told, and one that Paul learned from them. They accompanied the telling of this story with a cultic meal which developed into the Eucharist. Gospel and Eucharist, a story and a meal of thanksgiving, appear to have been essential marks of some of those little communities from their beginning, or at least from before Paul's adhesion to the movement. This study will focus on that story and how it took shape.

1. Martin Hengel estimates that Paul joined the Jesus movement within a year and a half to three years of Jesus' crucifixion (*The Pre-Christian Paul* [London: SCM Press; Philadelphia: Trinity Press International, 1991], 63).

2. I use "gospel" with a lowercase *g* to refer to the story, "the good news," and reserve the uppercase for the documents that rehearse the story in a much expanded form, that is, for the Gospels of Mark, Matthew, Luke, and John.

3

Some of the first members had been followers of Jesus of Nazareth, and the story they told centered on the end of his life. There may have been other communities whose founding members had been followers of Jesus and who told other stories about him, but this study will concentrate on those who told the story that Paul repeated. It was certainly about Jesus, but it had not been learned by following his activities or listening to his teaching in Galilee. Indeed, in the condensed form that Paul rehearses, Jesus was not even given his own name. That condensed story, as reported by Paul twenty to twenty-five years later, was "that Christ died for our sins in accordance with the scriptures, that he was buried, that he was raised on the third day in accordance with the scriptures, and that he appeared to Cephas, then to the twelve" (1 Corinthians 15:3-5). A fundamental question, which this study will explore, is: what are the origins of this story?

What became of this little Jewish movement with its story and its cult is well known, however: the movement expanded in time, becoming the Christian church, and its story, augmented by reflection on it and by other stories about Jesus, was expanded into the writings of the New Testament and of the early Church Fathers. The expansion resulted largely from the movement's inclusion of non-Jewish members, a practice that contributed to its separation from its original context, that of the Jewish people. The separation probably arose over a number of issues, in a variety of places and at different times,[3] but the break was definite within a hundred years, and relations were growing ever more acrimonious.

My question is not about what resulted from the formulation of the story, however, but about the formulation or discovery itself. Where did the story come from? What accounts for its specific formulation, as reported by Paul? How did the followers of Jesus

3. On this see James D. G. Dunn, *The Partings of the Ways between Christianity and Judaism and Their Significance for the Character of Christianity* (London: SCM; Philadelphia: Trinity Press International, 1991).

come to tell it in the form we find in verses 3, 4, and 5 of the fifteenth chapter of Paul's first letter to the Corinthians? I take this question to be in the first place a historical one.

It is also a biblical question, if the term "biblical" includes how Jews in the first century of the Common Era read and understood their Bible. Since the striking phrase "according to [or in accordance with] the scriptures" occurs at no less than two points, and since the authors of this gospel were Jews, any answer must depend upon understanding how Jews read their scriptures at this time. My question, then, concerns Jewish exegesis or interpretation some thirty-five years before the outbreak of the Jewish war of independence that ended with the Roman capture of Jerusalem and the destruction of the Temple.

The question also has a theological aspect, however, but one that is partly independent of the religious commitments of those who seek to answer it. Any answer will not only have to include some account of the god[4] who is implied in the story or gospel, but will also reveal, in the respondent's account of the story's origins, his or her own understanding of god. Thus we must consider both what sort of god the gospel presupposes, and also what sort of god is presupposed in any account of how it was formulated. I think it is possible to answer the first of these questions, if not the second, apart from one's religious commitments.

Since this investigation concerns the prejudices or presuppositions of the discoverers of the gospel, it is especially important that we recognize our own prejudices. We shall be considering the origins of Christianity and, therefore, the beginnings of the Christian-

---

4. Since N. T. Wright has reminded us, as Paul reminded the community in Corinth, that there were "many gods and many lords" (1 Corinthians 8:5) in the Hellenistic world of the first century, I follow his example of using the word with a lowercase *g* unless the god in question is fully specified. See N. T. Wright, *The New Testament and the People of God* (Minneapolis: Fortress, 1992), xiv-xv. The God of Israel was one of, and rather different from, the many gods of that time — and of ours.

Jewish conflict, and this involves delving into the minds of pre-modern thinkers. Scarcely anyone could enter these matters without some prejudice, be they orthodox or liberal Christians, orthodox or liberal Jews, Enlightenment or post-Enlightenment humanists, or any combination of these identities. These observations are not intended to hide my own presuppositions. On the contrary, the nature of the question makes it imperative to lay all presuppositions on the table, those of the author and also those of the reader, and submit them to examination. So let me be as honest as I can about mine, while I ask the reader to do the same.

I am a Christian, first by birth and upbringing, then by conviction, and finally by critical reflection. But I am a Christian who has become aware of a living Jewish tradition. Since this discovery ran counter to central features of the theological tradition that I had been taught, I set about reconstructing how Christian theology might look if it incorporated an acknowledgment of the Jewish people as continuing, living Israel. I have been at this task ever since.

I am also a child of the Enlightenment, but one who insists on holding up for critical scrutiny every tenet by which the Enlightenment criticized previous understandings of the past and present. This includes any prejudice that tries to tell us that "facts" exist independently of interpretation.[5] Perhaps this statement, without further elaboration, will encourage the reader to face up to her or his own prejudices in approaching the inevitably self-involving question addressed in this study.

Finally, the historical question, whence came the early gospel of 1 Corinthians 15:3-5, also bears on Christian practice. However it is answered, the answer will touch on Christian and Jewish identities and on the difference between them. This will generate some view of the past and present relationship of the church to the Jewish

5. I owe my loosening from this prejudice in part to William James's lectures on *Pragmatism*, especially lecture seven, "Pragmatism and Humanism."

people and some judgment of the relations that ought to exist between Christians and Jews today.

By defining my question as primarily historical, I do not deny that it can be answered by an appeal to revelation. One could say that the early gospel was revealed by God to Peter and his companions, either by a heavenly voice, in a dream, or by some other divine intervention. But even with such an answer, the historical question would remain: by what human means did such a revelation take place? This concerns the human words in which the gospel was formulated. What, in the realm of human thought and activity, lies behind and led to precisely the formulation that Paul said he received?

The question is sharpened by a distinction made in Paul's earlier letter to the Thessalonians. There he thanked God for the fact "that when you received the word of God which you heard from us, you accepted it not as the word of men but as what it really is, the word of God" (1 Thessalonians 2:13). The question is not the self-identifying one, whether the early gospel of 1 Corinthians 15:3-5 "really is" a divine revelation, "the word of God." To tell the truth, I think it is, but this does not answer the essential question. What I want to understand is how the message came to be formulated, that is, the origin of those "words of men" that Paul heard other human beings speak and that, in their words or in his revision, he passed on to his hearers and readers.

The answer that I propose takes the form of a tentative historical reconstruction. This will be the subject of Part I, "The Gospel of the Scriptures." I can argue for no more than a hypothesis, since the sources for any reconstruction are quite limited. If more than a hypothesis is demanded, then the wisest answer is "We don't know." The hypothesis is this: that the gospel of 1 Corinthians 15:3-5 was the result of a creative application to the death of Jesus, and to indescribable occurrences that followed, of particular postbiblical Jewish interpretations of Israel's scriptures. Of first importance was the story known in the Jewish tradition as the *aqedah,* the binding

7

of Isaac. In short, the gospel was an interpretation of the execution of Jesus and the following events, shaped by current Jewish readings of their scriptures.

Although the hypothesis cannot be proved, attention to the historical context of the early gospel renders the hypothesis at the least plausible. A plausible account of the origin is better than none, and this hypothesis offers an explanation of how that gospel could have come to be formulated. It also shows why its discoverers claimed that it was "according to the scriptures."[6]

If the hypothesis is in any way accurate, it also throws a fresh light on the important matters that will concern us in Part II, "The Scriptures of the Gospel." First, it shows the continuity of the traditions of ancient Israel in their postbiblical Jewish interpretations and in the assertions of the Christian church. It brings to light both the indissoluble connection between the two parts of the church's Bible and the priority of its Old Testament. Second, the hypothesis demonstrates that Judaism and Christianity are grounded in two different interpretations of the same tradition. Defining the difference between the two traditions as one of interpretation does not diminish that difference but, rather, opens the possibility of attending to both interpretations, of following one without forgetting the other. It invites us to a dual reading of Israel's scriptures that does justice to and testifies to God's providential will to preserve two bearers of Israel's tradition into the present.

To return to our starting point, I can offer no more than a hypothesis in answer to the basic question. The objection can always

---

6. For a different assessment, see Raymond E. Brown, *The Death of the Messiah*, 2 vols. (New York: Doubleday, 1994), 2:1435-44 ("Appendix VI: The Sacrifice of Isaac and the Passion"). While granting that "obviously there are parallels between the redemptive sacrifice of Jesus and *Aqedah* theology of the redemptive sacrifice of Isaac" (1435), Brown still finds such parallels "very much on the implicit level" and "very subtle" (1441). Brown, who was looking for the influence of the *aqedah* primarily on the passion narratives, rather than on the pre-Pauline gospel, would presumably reject my hypothesis as too conjectural.

be made that we simply cannot know for sure. I respect the historian's concern to distinguish what can be firmly established on the basis of reliable evidence from what cannot, but I find the objection finally unsatisfactory, for it leaves us with no account of the origin of the gospel of 1 Corinthians 15:3-5. Other objections could also be made, but they would depend either on a debatable concept of divine intervention in human affairs or a better description of the context in which that gospel originated.

This context, we shall find, consists of a few "bare facts" that I believe are not disputed, together with a rich, but debatable, framework. Before the facts and the framework can be considered, however, it is necessary to examine the language of the gospel that Paul said he received.

CHAPTER 1

The Gospel before Paul

THERE WAS INDEED a gospel before Paul, despite the claim of the publishers of *The Lost Gospel Q* that "Q" was "the very first Gospel" and "older than the Christian church itself."[1] If there ever was such a written document as "Q," one would have to question whether it should be called a Gospel. Furthermore, it could hardly have been older than the Christian church, for who would have written it? In contrast to such claims, the existence of a formulation called "the gospel" within a few years of the death of Jesus and before Paul joined the Jesus movement is attested by Paul's explicit assertion that he had received such a gospel.

Verses 3, 4, and 5 of 1 Corinthians 15 are the most explicit, but not the only, evidence for a pre-Pauline Christian teaching. At several places in his letters, Paul seems to be reciting and possibly editing the words of other preachers. An example is the opening of his letter to the community in Rome, announcing

---

1. I quote from an order form distributed by the publisher of *The Lost Gospel Q: The Original Sayings of Jesus.* Consulting editor, Marcus Borg. Introduction, Thomas Moore. Editors, Mark Powelson and Ray Riegert (Berkeley, Calif.: Ulysses Press, 1996).

the gospel of God, which he promised beforehand through his prophets in the holy scriptures, the gospel concerning his Son, who was descended from David according to the flesh and designated Son of God in power according to the Spirit of holiness by his resurrection from the dead, Jesus Christ our Lord. (Romans 1:1b-4)

Another example is the lyric passage in the second chapter of his letter to the congregation in Philippi, which most scholars take to have been, or to be based on, an early hymn:

Christ Jesus, who, though he was in the form of God, did not count equality with God a thing to be grasped, but emptied himself, taking the form of a servant, being born in the likeness of men. And being found in human form he humbled himself and became obedient unto death, even death on a cross. Therefore God has highly exalted him and bestowed on him the name which is above every name, that at the name of Jesus every knee should bow, in heaven and on earth and under the earth, and every tongue confess that Jesus Christ is Lord, to the glory of God the Father. (Philippians 2:5b-11)

We shall return in Chapter 5 to these variations, both of which share with the gospel of 1 Corinthians the themes of humiliation and exaltation, but first we shall look closely at the text in 1 Corinthians 15.

"I delivered to you . . ." Paul says of the gospel he then rehearses, "what I also received." "Received" — Paul used this same verb earlier in the same letter (1 Corinthians 11:23-26) to speak of the cultic meal commemorating the supper "on the night when he [Jesus] was handed over." There he quotes the words of institution and says that he "received [them] from the Lord." He surely did not mean that the Lord had spoken to him in a dream or vision. In this context it is far more likely that Jesus was believed to have spoken those words and that they were handed on by his disciples. The same is true with the gospel of 15:3-5: Paul is transmitting what has been passed on to him.

11

In the letter to the Galatians (1:11), however, Paul insisted that the gospel he preached was not from any human being, that he did not receive it (again the same verb) from any human being, but that "it came through a revelation of Jesus Christ" (1:12). Does this mean that what he says in his letter to the Corinthians refers to a revelation, rather than a pre-Pauline gospel? I do not think so, but not primarily because of the polemical nature of the epistle to the Galatians, intended to establish Paul's authority independent of the leaders of the community in Jerusalem. More important is that these two texts demonstrate the dialectical character of Paul's thinking, which is clearly formulated in 1 Thessalonians. There he gives thanks to God because, as he says, "when you received the word of God which you heard from us, you accepted it not as the word of men but as what it really was, the word of God" (2:13).

I shall not presume to answer the question whether the gospel of 1 Corinthians 15 "really is . . . the word of God." A decision on the validity of this statement depends on the theological judgment of whether our concept of god allows that god sometimes acts in or through historical events. Since the answer depends on whether we think we can ever speak of a human action as also an act of god, we do not have to accept the polemical either/or of Galatians. We can say that the gospel, even as revelation, was also a human formulation.

The subject of the gospel that Paul received was *Christos*. Strictly speaking, *Christos* is merely the grammatical subject, for since the verbs "died" and "was raised" are in effect or actually passive, the true subject — the never visible, never self-evident agent — is God. As in the tales of the patriarchs of Israel, God's agency is a mystery to be detected, not in a divine hand manifestly intervening in this or that episode, but in the story as a whole. It is in fact, as Paul said in Romans 1:1, the gospel of God.

Nevertheless, the grammatical subject is *Christos*. The name Jesus does not appear at all, although it is present in the formulations of the early gospel in the other two epistles and especially

12

prominent in Philippians 2:5b-11. *Christos* is the Greek translation of the Hebrew word *māšîaḥ,* loosely transcribed in Greek as *messias* (hence the English translation "messiah") and literally meaning "anointed."

The time when scholars thought that this appellation tells us anything has passed. It is becoming ever clearer that in first-century Judaism the term *māšîaḥ* had no single accepted meaning. While a few passages of the New Testament (e.g., Luke 2:25-26; 3:15; John 1:41; 4:25) suggest that all good Jews were eagerly looking forward to the coming of the Messiah, who would in some way be the savior of his people, there is little to support this impression. Shemaryahu Talmon, one of the contributors to an international symposium on the subject, shows how the messianic idea evolved from an early political use connected with Israel's anointed kings, to its conceptualization in the period that concerns us and which is known as the Second Temple period, ending with the Temple's destruction in 70 c.e.[2] In fact, only four of the fifty-two extant pseudepigraphic Jewish documents of the period up to 135 c.e.[3] even contain the word, and only two say that the Messiah would be descended from David.[4] The conclusive view of all the participants in this symposium was that "Jews did not profess a coherent and normative messianology" [a teaching about the Messiah], and that "one can

2. S. Talmon, "The Concept of *Māšîaḥ* and Messianism in Early Judaism," in *The Messiah: Developments in Earliest Judaism and Christianity,* ed. James H. Charlesworth (Minneapolis: Fortress, 1992), 79-114, esp. 80-84.

3. I refer here to the collection of fifty-two documents assembled by James H. Charlesworth, ed., *The Old Testament Pseudepigrapha,* 2 vols. (New York: Doubleday, 1983-85). This is a wide-ranging collection of Jewish and Christian apocryphal literature from the Second Temple age and later, much of it pseudepigraphic (falsely ascribed to venerable figures of ancient Israelite history and lore), but much of it anonymous or pseudepigraphic only by later attribution. Most of these so-called pseudepigrapha survive only in late Christian manuscripts; many of them may be Christian documents.

4. J. H. Charlesworth, "From Messianology to Christology: Problems and Prospects," in *The Messiah,* ed. Charlesworth, 19-20.

no longer claim that most Jews were looking for the coming of the Messiah."[5]

The question arises why, then, of a number of possibilities, Jesus' followers chose this so unlikely title, when "it is becoming increasingly evident that there was little interest in a Messiah, Davidic or otherwise, let alone a standard messianic expectation."[6] Nevertheless, in a few documents, notably the *Psalms of Solomon* 17:21-32,[7] the Messiah is prominent as a royal figure: he is a King-Messiah. Since by the year 30 C.E. the land of Israel had for many years been occupied by the Romans, such a figure was inevitably political and subversive. If the Roman authorities could lay their hands on any would-be King-Messiah, they would naturally crucify him. Pilate evidently thought he had found one in Jesus, and crucify him he did.

As far as Christian texts are concerned, "the meaning of the title Messiah or *Christos* when applied to Jesus . . . was determined primarily by *Christian* conceptions of Jesus rather than by conventional *Jewish* messianic notions."[8] Although *Christos* was originally a title, by the time Paul learned the gospel it had become a name, and Paul uses it in this way. In Romans 9:5, he does use "the Christ" as a title, but this is the only place; he uses the word without an article more than 260 times in his seven authentic letters.[9] The word

5. Charlesworth, "From Messianology to Christology," 35. I have left the messianic ideas of the Qumran communities out of account, but on this subject see L. H. Schiffman, "Messianic Figures and Ideas in the Qumran Scrolls," in *The Messiah,* ed. Charlesworth, 116-29. See also John J. Collins, *The Scepter and the Star: The Messiahs of the Dead Sea Scrolls and Other Ancient Literature* (New York: Doubleday, 1995).

6. R. A. Horsley, "'Messianic' Figures and Movements in First-Century Palestine," in *The Messiah,* ed. Charlesworth, 295.

7. A translation is available in *The Old Testament Pseudepigrapha,* ed. Charlesworth, 2:667. The translator, R. B. Wright, suggests (p. 641) a date between 70 and 45 B.C.E.

8. D. E. Aune, "Christian Prophecy and the Messianic Status of Jesus," in *The Messiah,* ed. Charlesworth, 410. The emphases are his.

9. Romans, 1 Corinthians, 2 Corinthians, Galatians, Philippians, 1 Thessalonians, and Philemon are universally agreed to be by Paul.

occurs alone a full 60 percent of the time, clearly as the name of Paul's Lord (whom he also calls "the Lord Jesus" or simply "Jesus" some twenty-seven times). Almost 40 percent of the time it occurs in the phrase-names "Jesus Christ" and "Christ Jesus." Paul's use conforms to the usage of the gospel he received: the title of Messiah was so closely associated with the person of Jesus that it served as his alias.

If we ask how this came about, we are led to the manner of and the reason for Jesus' death: his execution as a messianic pretender. There is no cause to doubt that the title, expressing the official charge against him and probably fastened to his cross, was "King of the Jews." The phrase is about as close a translation of *māšîaḥ* as one could expect from a Roman military authority, unconcerned about the fine points of the thought of the people they ruled. We could say that we owe to Pilate the now indissoluble connection between the name "Jesus" and the title King-Messiah, "Christ."

Jesus of Nazareth almost certainly did not make this connection himself. The Gospels portray him as singularly reticent about messianic claims made by his followers, and there is only the weakest of evidence that he claimed to be the Messiah. Furthermore, even indirect evidence is lacking: his "ministry of healing and teaching cannot . . . serve as the basis for the claim that he is the Messiah, . . . nor can the claim be derived from Jesus' own teaching and exegesis."[10]

The story in Mark 8:29-33 of Peter's confession on the way to Caesarea Philippi, "You are the Christ," suggests, in what is probably the oldest and certainly the shortest form of the story, an ironic explanation of Jesus' designation as Christ, namely, that although Jesus refused the title Messiah, Peter clung to it so strongly that Jesus had to call him Satan. It is plausible to think that Peter,

---

10. Donald Juel, *Messianic Exegesis: Christological Interpretation of the Old Testament in Early Christianity* (Philadelphia: Fortress, 1988), 25.

and perhaps others, believed that Jesus really was the Messiah and that word of this conviction circulated and eventually reached the Romans through their spies. In which case we could conclude that it was the faith of Peter and others that led to Jesus' arrest, conviction, and death.[11] The mysterious event on the first day of the week would have convinced the disciples that Peter had been right after all to insist on Jesus' identity as the Messiah. The difficulty with this reconstruction, however, is that it requires that we read the story of Peter's denial of Jesus (Mark 14:66-72), which consists in *not* acknowledging Jesus, as a cover-up of the greater sin of betrayal: Jesus is betrayed to the Romans, not by Judas, but by Peter's faith. This is not an impossible reading, but it calls for a level of irony that may lie beyond even that of Mark.[12]

If the explanation of why Jesus was first called Messiah lies neither in his conduct, actions, or teaching, nor in that of his disciples (note that not one of them was arrested by the Romans), it cannot be found in Jesus' resurrection, either. As Donald Juel says, "Jesus' resurrection by itself would have convinced no one that he was the Messiah, since no one expected the Messiah to die or to be raised from the dead."[13] (The point is valid even though there would have been no gospel at all if Jesus' disciples had not interpreted whatever happened on Easter as a resurrection.) It is better, therefore, to follow Juel in accepting the conclusion of Nils Dahl,[14] that it

11. Cf. William Nicholls, *Christian Antisemitism: A History of Hate* (Northvale, N.J.: Jason Aronson, 1993), 83: "one problem [Jesus] could not overcome: the misplaced enthusiasm of his own followers. This, not Jewish rejection, led to his death."

12. "The reader of current interpretations of New Testament texts from a literary critical point of view will find discussions of irony to be pervasive." So Burton L. Mack, *A Myth of Innocence: Mark and Christian Origins* (Philadelphia: Fortress, 1988), 338 n. 3.

13. Juel, *Messianic Exegesis*, 25.

14. Nils Alstrup Dahl, *Jesus the Christ: The Historical Origins of Christological Doctrine*, ed. Donald H. Juel (Minneapolis: Fortress, 1991), 27-47. The essay, "The Crucified Messiah," was first published in 1961. Not all agree, of course, but Dahl's argument is careful and, I believe, persuasive.

was precisely Jesus' execution as a King-Messiah which fixed a connection between his name and person on the one hand and the title and office of Messiah on the other. However, while images of and the theme of royalty fill the passion narratives, there is nothing royal in the bare facts of Jesus' arrest, conviction, and execution by the Romans, precisely the foreign rulers that a King-Messiah was supposed to overcome in restoring Israel to freedom under God alone in the Land of Promise. Indeed, Jesus' humiliating and disgraceful end was so contrary to what little Jewish messianic expectation there may have been that we are left with Pilate's charge affixed to the cross, "King of the Jews," as the reason why he came to be called Christ.

Another point should be made about this title. While the conviction that Jesus was the King-Messiah precisely as one crucified may have been the chronological starting point of the Christian movement, it never became the center of Christian faith. As Juel puts it, following Dahl, the messianic claim was the presupposition, not the content, of the gospel. If the disciples had not become convinced that Jesus was the Messiah, they would not have adapted the interpretation of certain biblical texts, read as messianic by other Jews before them, to form the early gospel. The fact is, however, that Paul asked his Gentile converts to confess Jesus Christ as Lord, not as Messiah.[15] The shift in the use of Messiah had taken place already: "Christ" had already become a name, and so it has remained.

The gospel Paul received contains puzzle upon puzzle. Its opening words, "Christ died," confront us with a strident oxymoron, or contradiction in terms: the Messiah was not supposed to die, at least not before a ripe old age. A man who died at the hands

---

15. Although one might argue that *kyrios,* "Lord," would have had more meaning for Gentiles than the biblical term "anointed," Paul writes as though his Gentile readers had some familiarity with the Bible in its Greek translation, the Septuagint.

of Israel's enemies could hardly have been the Messiah. At the same time, the next three words, "for [*hyper*] our sins," suggest, without any explanation, something of great moment. "The formula with *hyper*, either in the form 'for us' or 'for our sins,' is common in Paul's letters. It appears [also] in statements about Jesus' death in Hebrews, in 1 Peter, and in the Gospel accounts of Jesus' last meal with his followers. The phrase is never explained. Paul assumes his readers understood what it means."[16]

Juel suggests that the source of the idea of atonement that Paul seems to have had, and which may have been held by those who gave him this gospel, may lie in the next words: "according to the scriptures." But in order to understand this phrase, as well as the preceding one, "died for our sins," we must remember that the first disciples were first-century Jews. Whatever ideas they had in mind must have been available within their Second Temple Jewish context, and we shall explore these in Chapter 4.

The phrase "according to the scriptures" is evidently important, since it is repeated in connection with the resurrection. On the face of it, an appeal to the scriptures looks as absurd as Jewish and other critics of the church's gospel have always said. How could anyone familiar with the Bible of the Jewish people claim that "Christ died for our sins in accordance with the scriptures?" Yet this is what those early sectarian Jews did say, and we can be fairly sure that they knew their scriptures. Of course we shall need to learn what they meant by "the scriptures," and especially their method of interpreting them. We shall consider this in the next chapter with the aid of Juel's excellent introduction to the art of first-century Jewish exegesis.[17]

The early gospel added that Christ "was buried" and that, after he was raised (on the third day in accordance with the scriptures), "he appeared to Cephas, then to the twelve." The significance of these matched elaborations is not clear. Are they supposed to show

16. Juel, *Messianic Exegesis*, 6.
17. Juel, *Messianic Exegesis*.

that he actually died and so was truly raised? This would reflect a more apologetic attitude than the church was likely to have had at this early stage in its history. To say that the confused and frightened followers of Jesus turned to the scriptures in order to prove a point assumes that they already understood their gospel and used the scriptures in the hope of persuading skeptics. It is much more likely, however, that they were trying to deal with the oxymoron "crucified Messiah," the painful enigma of Jesus crucified as King of the Jews. To do so, they turned to the one source of wisdom available to and acknowledged by first-century Jews, their scriptures.

The phrases "he was buried" and "he appeared to Cephas, then to the twelve" could reflect some knowledge of the events of that Passover weekend.[18] There may have existed an early testimony that Jesus' tomb was found empty, and this could have led to a conviction that Jesus had been raised by God and to the experiences of his "appearing." Such a testimony could also have inspired the slightly different belief that the crucified Jesus had been exalted to "the right hand of God" (Philippians 2:9; Hebrews 1:3), for the story of Jesus' ascension probably reflects a different early interpretation of God's affirmation, rather than (as Luke presents it) a second event following the resurrection. On the other hand, some of the appearances may have come first and inspired the conviction that the tomb was empty. The fact that Mark, the earliest of the written Gospels, tells the story of the empty tomb first is counterbalanced by the fact that Paul, by far the earliest of all the written sources, never even mentions it. The tradition of a first appearance to Peter, found in the pre-Pauline gospel and repeated in Luke's Emmaus story (24:35), is a strong argument for the second alternative. Indeed, the special place of Peter and the Twelve in the early church may be rooted in a story of the appearances that are listed in 1 Corinthians 15:5.

18. *Cephas* (Aramaic) or *Petros* (Greek) (both mean "Rock") was the nickname for the Jew Shimon Bar Iona — Simon, son of Jonah — better known today as Peter, prominent among the disciples of Jesus of Nazareth (Matthew 16:16-19).

According to the early gospel, Jesus was raised on the third day in accordance with the scriptures, but the actual event may have occurred on a later day or over a period of time. To a person trained in biblical language, "the third day" speaks not of days and hours but of God's gracious mercy after a time of trial,[19] as in Hosea 6:2: "After two days he will revive us; on the third day he will raise us up." "On the third day" was when "Abraham lifted up his eyes and saw the place" where he was to offer up his beloved son Isaac (Genesis 22:4). Further, "On the third day, as morning dawned, there was thunder, and lightning, and a dense cloud upon the mountain, and a very loud blast of the horn; and all the people who were in the camp trembled. Moses led the people out of the camp toward God . . ." (Exodus 19:16-17, JPS). This conventional meaning of "the third day" may have shaped the first chronology of the end of Jesus' life in Mark's passion narrative. There we hear of Jesus' crucifixion on a Friday ("the day before the Sabbath," 15:2) and his resurrection on the following Sunday ("the first day of the week," 16:2). By the time of the mid-second-century church manual known as the *Didache,* or of the late first-century manual from which it might have been taken,[20] "the Lord's Day," presumably Sunday, has become the proper time to celebrate the Eucharist (*Didache* 14:1). I shall continue to speak of Easter and of "the first day of the week," even while recognizing that the event may have happened later or over a period of time.[21]

Whatever occurred on the first day of the week after Jesus' execution, the last verse of Mark's Gospel suggests that the occur-

---

19. Pinchas Lapide, *The Resurrection of Jesus: A Jewish Perspective* (Minneapolis: Augsburg, 1983), 92.

20. For a discussion of the dating, see Cyril C. Richardson, trans. and ed., *Early Christian Fathers,* Library of Christian Classics, vol. 1 (Philadelphia: Westminster, 1953), 162-66.

21. John Dominic Crossan, *Jesus: A Revolutionary Biography* (San Francisco: HarperSanFrancisco, 1994), 159, entitles his last chapter "How Many Years Was Easter Sunday?"

rence was as frighteningly incomprehensible to the disciples as the cross: "And [the three women] went out and fled from the tomb; for trembling and astonishment had come upon them; and they said nothing to any one, for they were afraid" (Mark 16:8).[22] The empty tomb was evidently no cause for relief. It would only become a consolation after it had been interpreted according to the scriptures. At the same time, if the Easter event consisted first of all in the appearances, or even in a sense of Jesus' presence, these were as unsettling (Luke 24:37) as the empty tomb.

An empty tomb itself is ambiguous. Someone might have taken the body. Perhaps the disciples could not find the tomb, for the body had been buried by Joseph of Arimathea, not by them (Mark 15:43, 46). Luke writes that the apostles dismissed the first report of the empty tomb as "an idle tale, and they did not believe" (24:11). As to the appearances, the same evangelist says (24:37) that the disciples thought they saw "a spirit." Matthew says that "some doubted" (28:17), and the Fourth Gospel explains this by saying that "as yet they did not know the scripture that he must rise from the dead" (John 20:9). Whatever happened to Jesus and among his disciples on the first day of the week needed interpretation even more than did his execution. Both events became good news only when the disciples discovered how to interpret them.

Thus, the Easter gospel could have arisen in three possible ways. The first is that the discovery of a new and positive way in which to speak of Jesus' death and of Jesus after his death, that is, a new way of perceiving Jesus, was itself the event of Easter. The second possibility is that the empty tomb was interpreted as evidence of his resurrection or ascension to the right hand of God. The third possibility is that some indescribable vision was understood as an appearance of Jesus alive after his death. Whether the shock that

22. The consensus is that Mark's Gospel ended at 16:8, with the following verses (printed as footnotes in the RSV) being drawn from the other Gospels and added later.

forced the disciples to search the scriptures was augmented by an event interpreted as an empty tomb, by events interpreted as appearances, or by both, we can be sure that the shock was caused first of all by his crucifixion as "King of the Jews." A decision for the second or third possibilities would add to the list of presumed historical facts behind the gospel, but it does not change the basic fact that the gospel and, so, Christian faith and the Christian church are built on an interpretation of these presumed facts in accordance with the scriptures. Since the presumed resurrection is a symbol, an interpretation (and this must be stressed), a Christian can speak of the Easter event without deciding among the possibilities.

So, here is the content of the gospel that the movement had formulated by the time that Paul joined it: Christ (a name for Jesus) died for our sins and was buried, and was raised on the third day and appeared, all this "according to the scriptures." What this message was supposed to mean and how it could be good news lie in the less than self-evident phrase "according to the scriptures."

CHAPTER 2

The Context

To UNDERSTAND THE DISCOVERY or invention of the pre-Pauline gospel, we must first know the circumstances of its discoverers and see them in the situation in which they arrived at their formulation. Their situation was determined by a few facts and shaped by patterns of thought and behavior characteristic of their world. The known facts are few in number. First and foremost is one that is not disputed but often so taken for granted as to be virtually ignored. As we shall see, it is the key that opens up every other feature of the context: *the discoverers of the pre-Pauline gospel were all Jews.*

The immediate and broader contexts of these Jews are important. The discoverers were members of the small group of Jews who had been closely associated with the Jewish teacher and healer, Jesus of Nazareth. They had undoubtedly been so impressed by Jesus that they followed him from Galilee up to Jerusalem, perhaps fixing on him their hopes for God's deliverance of their people from Roman occupation. Whatever their specific hopes, all hope was shattered by Jesus' arrest and crucifixion at the hands of the Romans.

We know little of that arrest and execution other than that they occurred. However, the tradition that Pilate had a sign attached to Jesus' cross, bearing some such words as "King of the Jews," seems more reliable than that the incident was invented. As I said in the previous chapter, "King of the Jews" was a reasonable Roman interpretation of the Hebrew *mašîaḥ,* "the anointed" one, the king for whom at least some Jews were longing. While it is difficult to determine whether Jesus' followers had previously thought that he might be the hoped-for king, it is fairly certain that Jesus was condemned by Pilate and executed as a would-be Messiah, since a royal pretender not chosen and empowered by the emperor would have been guilty of lèse majesté anywhere in the Roman Empire.

It was also noted in the previous chapter that the claim or belief that Jesus was the Messiah was not a part of the early gospel, but its presupposition. Jesus was simply named "Messiah," for the gospel Paul learned opens with the words "*Christ* died for our sins." It was the title on the cross, however Pilate meant it, that opened the possibility for Jesus' disciples to see him retrospectively as the Messiah.

We can take an uncertain step farther into the circumstances by saying that something astonishing occurred on the first day of the week after the execution. None of the disciples tried to describe it, but whatever happened, it appears to have left them as upset as the crucifixion. The disconcerting effect of the Easter event is less obvious to Christians than is that of the crucifixion, because they forget that "resurrection" is an interpretation that the disciples reached, either on that day or sometime later, not simply the standard name for a definable event. The Easter story, as variously told by the evangelists years later, presents the appearances as a series of epiphanies bearing their own interpretation. However, they also convey reports of fear and doubt, which make such a picture unlikely. The comment of John 20:9, "for *as yet* they did not know the scripture, that he must rise from the dead," suggests that whatever the events — appearances, visions, or the discovery of an empty tomb — they were not self-explanatory. The interpretation — "raised" (1 Corinthians 15:4, 20; Romans 4:25), "resurrection" (1 Corinthians 15:42; Romans 1:4), "ascended" (John 3:13; 6:62;

20:17; Ephesians 4:8, 10) — was not automatic. It was, in fact, revolutionary. But until it was found, the disciples had no cause for relief or joy. To summarize their situation: "they were afraid and said nothing to anyone" (Mark 16:8, my translation). We could hardly improve on Mark's concluding words.

The Christian movement is evidence enough that the disciples were rescued from their speechlessness, and its early literature gives ample clues as to how this came about. They found the words and symbols they needed by doing what any Jew of that time, at a loss for words to speak of a shocking experience, would have done. Instinctively they turned to the world they knew best, which they could trust and where God's will could be found, the world of their sacred scriptures.

Before we follow their journey, however, we need to be clear that the world they saw as trustworthy was not where it is for us. Most of us in the West at the close of the twentieth century think that what is real is to be found in the physical world, where history happens, not in the mind and not in books. "Out there" is where we think of god acting, if we think of a god at all and of a god as one who acts. If we think there is any divine purpose, we think it is being or will be unfolded "out there." That is where human life and whatever meaning it may have are played out, where the game of life is won or lost.[1] It is as natural for us, as it would have been foreign to those Jews, to look to the historical life and teaching of Jesus as keys to understanding his death and Easter. For us, the expression "the gospel of Jesus Christ" is more liable to refer to the historically reconstructed message of a historical figure, Jesus of Nazareth, identified variously as a healer and preacher, a prophet of Jewish restoration, or a Galilean holy man or Hasid, than to the message rehearsed in 1 Corinthians 15:3-5. If we

---

1. As the image of a game suggests, "what we think" might be better called a pagan vision or understanding. On the role of sports in paganism, past and present, and their total absence from the biblical world and postbiblical Judaism, see Maurice Samuel, *The Gentleman and the Jew: Twenty-five Centuries of Conflict in Manners and Morals* (New York: Behrman House, 1977), esp. Book One.

attempt to move from the historical Jesus to that gospel, or conversely from the gospel that Paul received to that historical Jesus, we run into difficulties. Neither of these moves was contemplated by the formulators of the gospel. Instead, they went from the death of the "King of the Jews" (perhaps also from the occurrences of Easter) to their scriptures, back and forth, until they found both a meaning for those events, which they called the good news, and a new meaning for those scriptures. If we ignore this procedure, failing to see that their distinctive test for truth was in the scriptures, our twentieth-century minds may try to find a connection between the early gospel and the Jesus of Nazareth detectable by historical research, but we shall discover only the feeblest of connections. A stronger link will appear when we include in the equation the test of reality characteristic of first-century Jews.

There is no need to imagine the disciples retiring to a *Beth Midrash* and poring over texts. For all we know, they may have been unable to read. But as Jews they would have heard the Torah read again and again, and not only in a synagogue. Apart from instruction from parents, there were the Pharisees. There were also the many priests, only a few of whom would have been on duty in the Temple at any time. The vast majority would have been in their villages, teaching Torah, as traditionally required, to their neighbors.[2] For first-century Jews the first meaning of the phrase "the oral Torah," an expression later applied to the Mishnah and Talmud, would have been the scriptures and their interpretation, read aloud and discussed.

The worldview of these Jews was shaped by Israel's great story, unfolded in the Torah, appealed to in the Prophets, and celebrated and rehearsed in the Psalms. Even for so Hellenized a Jew as the philosopher Philo, this story was the foundation of his thought. Even Israel's Wisdom tradition, which often sounds so Hellenistic,

2. On the teaching function and number of priests in Israel, see the article "Priests and Priesthood" in *Encyclopedia Judaica,* vol. 13, especially columns 1079-80 and 1085.

was molded by it. The story was of Israel under its god, creator of the heavens and the earth, who had chosen this people to be his special possession and his instrument for dealing with all the nations. This story contained the truth about God and the truth about the world; it was the key to all mysteries. For the first followers of Jesus, it was the only place to look in their distress. In fact, we know that they turned to it, for they found the way out of their speechlessness by telling the story of Jesus, especially the most baffling part, his end, as Israel's story. They told his story in the idiom of Israel.

The times were difficult for the Jewish people. Their forebears had been carried off as prisoners to Babylon, leaving the ruins of their capital city. Although many were allowed to return within two or three generations, when Babylon was overthrown by the Persians under Cyrus, Jerusalem remained under Persian control. The Jerusalem temple was rebuilt in 520-515 B.C.E., and Palestine passed to Ptolemaic and then Seleucid control before a measure of political independence, to some extent based on a treaty with Rome, was achieved under the Hasmoneans in 164 B.C.E. Independence was lost when Pompey captured Jerusalem in 63 B.C.E., and the Romans had ruled since that time. Caesar was now lord over Israel. While some found the arrangement bearable and some even profitable, many experienced it as blasphemous and cruel. Many had their eye on a better future, and those who wrote of it often used fabulous language. Their hope, however, was for this created world and especially for Israel, God's chosen historical people. It is important to keep this worldly framework in mind if we expect to understand the thinking of those Jews who used the unlikely word "resurrection" to speak of Jesus' new beginning.

For Jews of this time, the idea of a resurrection was intimately bound up with the restoration, rescue, or deliverance of the people Israel.[3] The idea was fluid, still being developed, but one of its

---

3. On this, see N. T. Wright, *The New Testament and the People of God* (Minneapolis: Fortress, 1992), 200-201, 320-32.

27

important functions was to answer the question, Who will be present to celebrate when the land of Israel is delivered from foreign domination? Would the faithful and loyal Jews who died before that day be included? The Jewish hope in a resurrection has less to do with survival or new life after death than with sharing in the restoration and rescue of God's elect. A reflection of this conception and the question it answered is found in the colorful language of 1 Thessalonians, perhaps Paul's earliest extant letter, where he assures his readers that they need not grieve for the faithful who have died, for they will be raised up to meet the Lord in the day of his coming (4:13-17).

Resurrection, the hope of the dead being raised, was therefore primarily a social and political concept, part of the Jewish hope for the long-awaited end of exile and foreign domination. Consequently, the idea of a general resurrection was congenial to the Pharisees, an essentially lay and democratic movement, close to the people and their hopes. It was rejected by the Sadducees, a more aristocratic movement inclined to cooperate with the Roman occupation.

It is not so easy to understand why this idea was seized upon by the disciples as appropriate to the event on the first day of the week. Confronted, let us suppose, with the appearance of their dead master alive on that "first day of the week," those frightened Jews would probably not have thought of a resurrection. The rescue from foreign control which gave the word its meaning was starkly absent, and whatever the disciples may have witnessed on "the first day of the week" had no feature that could encourage the use of the term. The word "resurrection" does not occur in the Gospel accounts of Easter morning, the usual term being the one in the gospel of 1 Corinthians 15:3-5, "raised." Jesus was raised, or raised from the dead, or is risen, but since this is only another way of speaking of resurrection, even this use is puzzling.

Thus, the context of the discovery of the early gospel was the shock of the crucifixion of Jesus of Nazareth as "King of the Jews," and perhaps the aftershock of the appearances, or the finding of the empty tomb, or both, experienced through the worldview that was articulated in Israel's story. The background of the discovery was a conviction that the scriptures which mediated Israel's story were the most reliable test of truth. Since the gospel of 1 Corinthians 15, backed by the other early traditions, singles out Peter, the spokesman for the apostles (Mark 8:29; 9:5-7; and their parallels), as the first to whom the risen Jesus appeared (Luke 24:34), we may guess that he was the first of the disciples to formulate something like that gospel. He would thus have interpreted Jesus primarily on the basis of his end: his death and resurrection. Mark 8:28 reveals that there were other interpretations which did not focus on Jesus' end: some saw Jesus as John the Baptist returned, as Elijah, or as one of the prophets. These interpretations were also shaped by Israel's story, but they took no account of the shocking end of Jesus' life. Such interpretations, however, could hardly have been adequate for those who had deserted him at his arrest, possibly seen his execution from afar, and then seen him in a whole new way "on the first day of the week." What they needed, and what was found perhaps first by Peter, was a view of Jesus that fully incorporated his death as "King of the Jews" and that was in accordance with the scriptures. Our next task is to follow them in their search of the scriptures to discover the meaning of that death.

CHAPTER 3

"According to the Scriptures"

IN ATTEMPTING TO FOLLOW Jesus' disciples in their anguished search into the one trustworthy source of understanding, the scriptures of Israel, we must keep in mind that a text, specifically a biblical text, was not for them or for any other Jew of the time what it is for us. For us a text is a window onto events or into persons and their thoughts and attitudes. Our interest lies primarily in that which lies behind a text.[1] First-century Jews, so scholars of the period tell us, saw reality lying directly in the text itself.[2]

The idea of the centrality of, nay, the exclusive validity of, the text as the locus of divine wisdom, instruction, and revelation was not invented by first-century Judaism. It already characterized Ezra's reform of Jewish life and practice following the return from Babylon which would develop into the rabbinic principle: no more prophecy

---

1. We tend "to ignore what is written in favor of what is written about" (Frank Kermode, *The Genesis of Secrecy: On the Interpretation of Narrative* [Cambridge: Harvard University Press, 1979], 118-19, attributing the phrase to Jean Starobinski).

2. For this and what follows, see Donald Juel, *Messianic Exegesis: Christological Interpretation of the Old Testament in Early Christianity* (Philadelphia: Fortress, 1988), esp. Chap. 2.

after Ezra.[3] Well before the first century, it became the established practice and understanding that if a Jew wanted to know the will of God on any matter, he would no longer seek out a prophet or rely on the omens of a Temple priest, as would have been normal in ancient Israel; now he consulted the text of the Torah or, better yet, a man versed in reading and interpreting the Torah. The word of God was no longer sought in prophetic utterance, but in the written words of the Book, the scriptures, and even more, in their interpretation in midrashim (narrative interpretations) and in relatively free scriptural translations.

First-century Jews saw the scriptures as a collection of God's words for the benefit of his people Israel and, through Israel, of the whole world. The words were given by God himself. We would call them oracles. Because each individual word was held to be thus inspired, it was thought right to associate one text with another on the sole basis of a word common to both of them. If one were puzzled by a particular word in a text, one would look for other texts that contained the same word. Those texts could be expected to solve the puzzling aspect of the word in the first text.

A lovely example of this method occurs in a document that, although later than the first century, appears to follow a well-established practice. A certain Rabbi Simon of Kitron noticed a puzzle in Psalm 114, the delicious rehearsal of the Exodus event, where the third verse says literally, "The sea saw and fled."[4] "Saw" *(rā'â)* calls for a direct object, a grammatical feature that is hidden by the usual translations. What, Rabbi Simon asked himself, did the sea

---

3. On the cessation of prophecy, see *Encyclopedia Judaica*, vol. 4, 823; cf. also 1 Maccabees 9:27. Cf. George Foot Moore, *Judaism in the First Centuries of the Christian Era: The Age of the Tannaim* (Cambridge: Harvard University Press, 1927-1930; reprint, New York: Schocken: 1971), 1:239, 358.

4. Juel, *Messianic Exegesis,* 43, found this in Jacob Z. Lauterbach, ed. and trans., *Mekilta de-Rabbi Ishmael: A Critical Edition,* 3 vols. (Philadelphia: Jewish Publication Society, 1973), 1:220. Burton Visotzky, *Reading the Book: Making the Bible a Timeless Text* (New York: Doubleday, 1991), 125 also deals with this text, giving Simon's name as "Shimeon."

see that caused it to flee *(nûs)?* Well, the Bible told of another flight: the righteous Joseph, resisting the seductions of his master's wife, who "caught him by his garment, saying, 'Lie with me' . . . left his garment in her hand, and fled [*nûs*] . . ." (Genesis 39:12). Indeed, the words "left his garment . . . and fled" are repeated three more times in Genesis 39, in verses 13, 15, and 18. Now, Exodus 13:19 tells us that Moses took the bones of the righteous Joseph with him out of Egypt, as Joseph had requested when he was dying (Genesis 50:25). What the sea saw, therefore, were the bones of Joseph, and it rewarded Joseph's righteous flight from Potiphar's wife by fleeing before the escaping children of Israel.

Another example from the same source is attributed to Rabbi Banaah.[5] Why did God command Moses to stretch out his hand and *split (bāqaʿ)* the sea (Exodus 14:16)? This is a strange thing to try to do with water. But Rabbi Banaah found the puzzling word in another text, the foundational text that will be the focus of our next chapter, the *aqedah* or the binding of Isaac. There we read that Abraham *split (bāqaʿ)* the wood for the burnt offering (Genesis 22:3). Abraham's incomparable obedience to the command to sacrifice his beloved son received its analogous reward in the moment of Israel's deliverance from the pursuing Egyptians, split for split!

The exegetes were doing more than satisfying their curiosity about what the sea had seen or how it was divided. Far more important, they found new confirmations of their trust in God's providential rule over the vast realm of scripture. No word of the scriptures is there by chance. Even its repetitions ensure that the solution to its puzzles will not be missed. This confirmed God's providential rule not only over the scriptures, but over the whole history of his people that these books tell.

---

5. I owe this reference to Lauterbach, *Mekilta de-Rabbi Ishmael*, 1:218, but both these examples appear in Shalom Spiegel, *The Last Trial: On the Legends and Lore of the Command to Abraham to Offer Isaac as a Sacrifice: The Akedah* (New York: Behrman House, 1967).

What appears at first sight to be only a theology of words, even of verbal correspondence, presupposing a doctrine of verbal inspiration, is at a deeper level a theology of Israel's identity as the people of God, and ultimately of God's sovereignty over the whole world. Israel may have enemies, but under this god she can know that she is ultimately safe. This sort of exegesis supported the faith of both the exegete and his whole people.

Turning from the general method to the particular case of the disciples' search for understanding, I am assuming that their probable starting point was the oxymoron "crucified Messiah."[6] If this is correct, we could assume that they looked first to the passages of scripture that we know from other Jewish sources were already understood to refer to the Messiah. The scrolls from the Qumran library establish that there were such messianic texts, of which the oracle of the prophet Nathan in 2 Samuel 7:10-14 was an important one. One of the Qumran exegetes seems even to have felt that he could take for granted an established eschatological, rather than a historical, reading of this important passage.[7] As the chart below, following Donald Juel's work, makes clear, the word "seed" was a key term (v. 12): David's seed, whose kingdom God established with his promise "I will be his father and he shall be my son" (v. 14).

6. This assumption is supported by the thesis of Nils Dahl, "The Crucified Messiah," in his collection of essays *Jesus the Christ: The Historical Origins of Christological Doctrine,* ed. Donald H. Juel (Minneapolis: Fortress, 1991), 27-47.

There is, however, scarcely a thesis on any point of biblical scholarship that is not contested, and this one is no exception. Donald Juel has called my attention to the astonishing objection of Brevard S. Childs, *Biblical Theology of the Old and New Testaments: Theological Reflection on the Christian Bible* (Minneapolis: Fortress, 1993), 229-30. Conceding that "Dahl's thesis has much to recommend it," Childs nevertheless objects that "it seems hardly adequate to attribute the origin of the Christian confession of Jesus as Messiah to the almost fortuitous (!) ascription of a messianic title by the Romans on the cross."

7. Juel, *Messianic Exegesis,* 76, discussing the *Florilegium* (or *Eschatological Midrashim*) from Qumran Cave 4. By contrast, a modern reading of the text would almost certainly be historical: David is promised a biological son and heir who will rule after him and build the Temple. Such indeed was Solomon.

The second Psalm was also read as a messianic text because it speaks explicitly of the LORD's *māšîaḥ*, his "anointed" (v. 2), and in v. 7 says that the LORD "said to me" (David being understood as the author), "You are my son, today I have begotten you." The links between these passages (highlighted in bold italics in chart A, p. 35) are "seed of David" and "son of God."[8] I have added the opening of Psalm 110, because its messianic interpretation is picked up in Mark 12:36-37 (and in Matthew 22:44-45 and Luke 20:42-43).[9]

Isaiah 11:1-3 and some lines from Zechariah and Jeremiah were likewise together read as messianic, the connection being made by moving from "branch" to "branch," as chart B (p. 36) shows.

Donald Juel has made the convincing proposal that Psalm 89 was quite probably the hinge on which the disciples' whole search into the scriptures turned.[10] (In the following excerpts from Psalm 89, the words that might have been picked up by a Jewish exegete of the scriptures in the first century, words already important in established messianic texts, are set in bold italics. In addition, other words that could have provided a vocabulary to speak of the humiliation of God's anointed, the Christ, are placed in regular italics.) Psalm 89 opens as a song of praise for the LORD's steadfast love and faithfulness to David's *seed* (v. 30), recalling God's covenant of eternal fidelity to David, his chosen one (v. 3), *servant* (vv. 3 and 20) and *anointed* one (v. 20). In the LORD's name "his horn shall be *exalted*" (v. 24). He shall cry to God as *his father* (v. 26), and, since David "*belongs to the LORD*" (v. 18), God will make of him God's "*first-born*, the highest of the Kings of the earth" (v. 27).

8. Note, however, the remark of Jon D. Levenson, *The Death and Resurrection of the Beloved Son: The Transformation of Child Sacrifice in Judaism and Christianity* (New Haven and London: Yale University Press, 1993), 207: "Here it is useful to remember that the relevance of a verse often extends beyond the words that the midrashist cites."

9. See Juel, *Messianic Exegesis,* 135-41 for a careful argument concluding that Psalm 110:1 "could be — and perhaps prior to the Christian era actually was — understood as messianic."

10. Juel, *Messianic Exegesis,* 104-6.

Texts read messianically by postbiblical Jews prior to Christianity

A: "Son (Seed) of David," "Son of God"

2 Samuel 7:11-14	Psalm 2:2, 6-8	Psalm 110:1
. . . the LORD will make you a house. 12 When your days are fulfilled and you lie down with your fathers, I will raise up your offspring [literally, *seed*] after you, who shall come forth from your body, and I will establish his kingdom. 13 He shall build a house for my name, and I will establish his kingdom for ever. 14 *I will be his father, and he shall be my son.*	2 . . . the rulers take counsel together, against the LORD and his *anointed.* . . . 6 I have set my king on Zion, my holy hill. 7 I will tell of the decree of the LORD: He said to me, "*You are my son,* today I have begotten you. Ask of me and I will make the nations your heritage." . . .	The LORD said to my lord, "Sit at my right hand, till I make your enemies your footstool."

But then in verse 38 this psalm of praise changes into one of agonizing lament over the psalmist's situation, for it appears that God has now *"rejected"* David and is "full of *wrath against* thy *anointed"* (v. 38). Covered with *shame* (v. 45), the LORD's *"servant is scorned"* (v. 50), and "the *anointed"* of the Lord is *taunted and mocked* (v. 51). In spite of the humiliations just recited, a concluding verse blesses the LORD, returning to the tone of the first thirty-seven verses.

35

B: From "Branch" to "Branch"

Isaiah 11:1-3	Zechariah 3:8; 6:12	Jeremiah 23:5; 33:15
1 There shall come forth a shoot from the stump of Jesse, and *a branch* shall grow out of his roots.	8 . . . I will bring *my servant the Branch.* . . .	5 Behold, the days are coming, says the LORD, when I will raise up for David a righteous *Branch,* and he shall reign as king. . . .
2 And the spirit of the LORD shall rest upon him, the spirit of wisdom and understanding . . .	12 . . . thus says the LORD of hosts, "Behold, *the man whose name is the Branch:* for he shall grow up in his place, and he shall build the temple of the LORD."	15 In those days and at that time I shall cause a righteous *Branch* to spring forth for David; and he shall execute justice and righteousness in the land.

The words highlighted in bold italics explain the importance of Psalm 89 at a very early stage of Christian messianic exegesis, and the psalm is alluded to over twenty times in the New Testament.[11] This is indeed a text that made it possible to speak of a crucified king of the Jews and to say that he is God's beloved "first-born," one ultimately "exalted." Psalm 89 also made it possible to regard the speaker of other psalms as the Messiah. Certainly later Jewish interpreters read Psalm 89 as messianic.[12] With its help, both the humiliation and the exaltation of the King-Messiah could be seen

11. Juel, *Messianic Exegesis,* 107.
12. Juel, *Messianic Exegesis,* 105-6 lists a number of passages from the midrashic tradition of the Rabbis.

and proclaimed as a part of God's reality, that is, according to the scriptures.

In addition, the opening verse of Psalm 110 may have been read by pre-Christian exegetes as referring to the exaltation of the King-Messiah. The Jews who began the Christian movement certainly made use of it to speak of the exaltation of Jesus to the right hand of God. However, the scriptural source for speaking of Jesus' exaltation is puzzling,[13] since neither Philippians 2 nor the opening verses of Romans has any reference to Psalm 110. A possible source for such language, however, will be explored in the next chapter.

13. As Juel, *Messianic Exegesis,* 150 acknowledges.

CHAPTER 4

From the Depths of the Scriptures

BEFORE DIGGING FOR THE DEEPER ROOTS of the early gospel of 1 Corinthians 15:3-5, it will be helpful to clear away some underbrush that clutters and obscures the ground. It has been argued that the root of the church's traditional anti-Judaism lies in the myth of the death and resurrection of Christ.[1] This myth is not only at odds with the teachings and actions of the Jew Jesus, which have been reconstructed by historical scholarship; it purports to offer a different and better religion than Judaism, which was the religion of Jesus as well as of his people. If we want to put anti-Semitism behind us, then, we should follow the Jew Jesus and his Jewish religion. The alternative, we are told, is to adhere to the story of Good Friday, Easter, and the Eucharist, in short, to traditional Christianity, which entails the repudiation of Judaism, the religion of Jesus the Jew.

It is true, of course, that Judaism and Christianity are based on different interpretations of Israel's tradition and that this led to

---

1. William Nicholls, *Christian Antisemitism: A History of Hate* (Northvale, N.J.: Jason Aronson, 1993), 3-15, elaborating the argument in the first four chapters and defining the options on 427-37.

conflict. It was naturally possible for Gentile Christians to misuse a message arising out of a Jewish interpretation of Israel's tradition to foster Christian anti-Judaism. How this difference might be seen and lived so as to avoid hostility and conflict is a matter to which I shall return in the second half of this study. This chapter will explore both the Jewish interpretation of a crucial piece of Israel's tradition and also its Christian application to Jesus, which together made the conflict possible and even likely, but which could also lead us to see the relationship between the church and the Jewish people as complementary.

Christianity probably existed in more than one form from a very early time. If so, the most influential configurations were, on the one hand, those that preserved or invented the story of the death and resurrection of Christ and practiced the cult of the sacred meal, and, on the other, congregations that preserved or invented collections of sayings attributed to Jesus and reports of his activities. Both of these approaches arose very early. Just as it appears that the story of the death and resurrection of Christ existed before Paul, an equally early date may be presumed for at least the beginnings of collections of Jesus' sayings. But whether or not the two traditions stemmed from separate groups of congregations, they were fused within less than forty years. To the dismay of some scholars,[2] the gospel of the death and resurrection became the controlling message, into which the sayings and acts of Jesus were integrated. This is the case in Mark and the later canonical Gospels; the early gospel also controls the various creeds, and its message is preserved in the theological tradition. The church's gospel has always been the story of the death and resurrection of him whose words and deeds are told in the four Gospels.

---

2. E.g., Burton L. Mack, *A Myth of Innocence: Mark and Christian Origins* (Philadelphia: Fortress, 1988), who is inclined to say that the myth and the cult were invented, whereas the sayings and teachings were preserved. I see no reason why the same verbs would not apply to the two bodies of materials and types of communities.

There is no question that the gospel of 1 Corinthians 15:3-5 is an interpretation of Jesus, but so are the historians' reconstructions of Jesus the Jew, Jesus the Galilean peasant, Jesus the wandering Cynic teacher of wisdom, or Jesus the charismatic. The interpretation of the primitive gospel, Jesus the crucified Messiah, raised by the power of God, is simply distinguished from the others in that it locates the significance of Jesus in his death. By contrast, the results of the various quests of the historical Jesus, from Reimaurus, who first attempted a critical historical life of Jesus in the eighteenth century, to the Jesus Seminar of today, share the characteristic of focusing on his life, rather than on his death (Mark 8:28 shows that to interpret Jesus without respect to his death is not just a modern predilection). The early gospel, however, has the merit of being the interpretation of some of Jesus' closest followers, as I noted in Chapter 1, quite possibly including Peter, and of having been adopted by Paul and by the authors of all the Gospels.

There is no objection to learning what critical historians, faced with such ancient, uncritical, and nonhistorical texts, can make of Jesus of Nazareth. In fact, my own hypothesis about how certain Jews came to say what they did about Jesus and the God of Israel depends on the conclusions of recent investigations. Although any such conclusions are necessarily hypothetical, some hypotheses are better than others. We should be quite clear, however, about the limitations that a method may impose upon the range of its search. One is the inability to investigate the divine. To expect historical research to tell us whether Jesus was God's Messiah is unreasonable.

What should not be done is to draw a sharp distinction between "the pre-Easter Jesus" of the historian and "the post-Easter Jesus" of Christian faith, calling the one human and the other divine.[3] Such a two-nature Christology contradicts the conviction

3. As does Marcus J. Borg, *Jesus in Contemporary Scholarship* (Valley Forge, Penn.: Trinity Press International, 1994), 171-72.

40

expressed in the early gospel, in all the Gospels, and in all the creeds, that it was precisely Jesus of Nazareth, the crucified one, who was raised to God's right hand. That assertion is the heart of the early gospel, and our quest is for its origin.

The early gospel may not contain a single self-evident clause, but it does contain the Christian *mythos* or story. How did it happen that the story was told in this particular way? Let me be clear about the question. In asking how Peter, or whoever first formulated the gospel, came to make these statements, I am not asking what may have stirred Peter to speak. What I want to know is why, once stimulated, he used just the phrases repeated by Paul. The use of "Christ," rather than "Jesus," may be explained, as we have seen, but why "for our sins"? Why "raised on the third day"? Above all, why the repeated phrase, "in accordance with the scriptures"? What is the source and meaning of this language?

Any Christian who agrees that the church needs to turn from its anti-Judaic past and acknowledge the enduring covenant of the Jewish people with God may find support in this language, for it is Jewish to the core, coming, as we shall see, from the very center of Jewish identity. By comparison, the Jewishness of the historical Jesus is almost irrelevant to the church's relations with the Jewish people for the reason that Christianity does not stand on the historical Jesus, but on the gospel. The gospel has a Jewish pedigree to which we should pay serious attention.

In the gospel that Paul learned, the key expression is "according to the scriptures." We should recall that for Jews of that time, the scriptures did not exist in the splendid (if unhistorical) isolation of the *sola scriptura* of the sixteenth-century Reformation. The Reformers taught, against the Catholic appeal to tradition, that the church should be governed on the sole basis of the Bible, with no appeal to later tradition. By contrast, at least some Jews, as scholars of the Qumran library have noted, accorded many documents that never made it into the biblical canon the same authority and treated them with the same respect as the books that were later accepted as canonical.[4] When I said that we could expect Jews of that time to have turned to the scriptures for understanding, it would have been more accurate to say that they turned to their tradition. This included not only the scrolls of the Hebrew Bible and the Septuagint, but also their interpretations of these texts.[5] The formulators of the gospel might as well have said, and Paul have written, "according to the traditions."

The citations and allusions throughout the New Testament show that many parts of the scriptures helped Peter and his colleagues to find their voices, providing words and images with which to tell themselves and others what had happened on that terrible Friday and on that unsettling *yom rishon* ("first day"). As we saw in the last chapter, Psalm 89 was probably an important stimulus. In it David, the presumed author, both praises God for his faithfulness and, explicitly as God's anointed, laments that he is scorned, mocked, cast off, and covered with shame.

Not every word of the primitive gospel was according to the Jewish scriptures; one term, as we have seen, probably originated in the text affixed to the cross on Pilate's orders. Ironically, the name that came to be joined permanently with that of Jesus, "Christ," may well be owed to his executioner. Apart from the name, however, the assertions that Christ died for our sins and was raised are said to be according to the scriptures. We shall find a possible source for these assertions in the radical Jewish reinterpretation, already evident in the first century C.E., of the story of the binding of Isaac (Genesis 22:1-19). In this story we are told not only that God commanded Abraham to sacrifice his beloved child of promise, but that Abraham was then promised abundant descendants, who would prosper in

---

4. See James C. VanderKam, *The Dead Sea Scrolls Today* (Grand Rapids: Eerdmans, 1994), 142-58.

5. Recent studies of postbiblical Jewish writings show the limitations of the attempt of C. H. Dodd, *According to the Scriptures* (London: Nesbit, 1952) to answer our question by reference to Israel's canonical literature alone.

turn, all "*because* you have *done* this, and *have not withheld* your son, your only son" (Genesis 22:16).

It should be noted that in the biblical story, God does not command Abraham to sacrifice the ram in place of Isaac. Abraham, stopped at the last moment by an angelic voice acknowledging his reverence for ("fear" of) God, looks about, sees the ram, and then offers it on the altar. Then a second angelic voice repeats God's blessing on Abraham and his seed. May we not assume that God accepted the replacement? The Rabbis in a later midrash (narrative interpretation) made clear that they knew the ram to have been only a replacement; the divine command was that Abraham sacrifice to God his beloved son. So they have Abraham praying: "Master of the Universe, regard it as though I had sacrificed my son Isaac first, and only afterwards sacrificed this ram."[6]

After such long-standing liberal assurances that this is not a story of child sacrifice, but a story told in order to abolish the practice, we need to hear Jon Levenson's argument that the story not only concerns the sacrifice of a child, as the Rabbis realized, but that the theme of the sacrifice of the beloved son runs throughout the tradition. This is especially evident in the Joseph story, where the very survival of the people threatened by famine depends on the willingness of the aging and sorrowful Jacob, who has already lost his first favorite son, Joseph, to give up his beloved Benjamin. To answer the objection that neither Joseph nor Benjamin actually dies, Levenson points out that Israel preserved a contrary tradition found in Jeremiah 31:15: "Rachel is weeping for her children; she refuses to be comforted for her children, because *they are not.*" Rachel's children were precisely Joseph and Benjamin.

Levenson argues that these stories reflect the explicit divine

---

6. *Genesis Rabbah* 56:9, cited by Jon D. Levenson, *The Death and Resurrection of the Beloved Son: The Transformation of Child Sacrifice in Judaism and Christianity* (New Haven and London: Yale University Press, 1993), 22. See further Shalom Spiegel, *The Last Trial: On the Legends and Lore of the Command to Abraham to Offer Isaac as a Sacrifice: The Akedah* (New York: Behrman House, 1967).

commandment, given with no means of circumvention in Exodus 22:28, "You shall give to Me the first-born among your sons" (JPS).[7] We are naturally tempted to supplement this text with the provision of Exodus 34:20 (evidently from another or later strand of the tradition), which not only allows for but actually prescribes the redemption of the firstborn son. There is no provision for a redemption in the earlier verse, however. We are not alone in wanting to qualify this stark commandment. In discussing Exodus 22:28, no less an authority than Rashi, the great eleventh-century Jewish commentator on the Bible, could not resist inserting the provision for a redemption that is conspicuous by its absence from this commandment.[8]

Levenson confronts us with further evidence that the firstborn son was sacrificed not only in the service of Molech among the Canaanites and the Carthaginians, but also in the worship of the God of Israel. The tirades of the later prophets Jeremiah — "I did not command them [to sacrifice their children], nor did it enter into my mind" (32:35) — and Ezekiel — "I [the LORD] gave them statutes that were not good and ordinances by which they could have life; and I defiled them through their very gifts in making them offer by fire all their first-born, that I might horrify them" (20:25-26) — certainly sound as if the practice continued among the Israelites, at least occasionally, until the Exile. And even when not practiced, child sacrifice remained a religious ideal. An ideal? Yes, Levenson argues, because perfect devotion to *Hashem* ("the Name" — an Orthodox Jewish circumlocution for the unutterable name of the God of Israel) could go as far as a willingness to give up, to sacrifice, what was most precious. The most precious belongs to God.[9]

7. So the Jewish Publication Society translation (JPS), where the verse numbering follows the Hebrew. The New American Bible (NAB) has the same numbering, but the verse is 29 in the Authorized Version (AV) and the Revised Standard Version (RSV).

8. A. M. Silbermann, *Chumash with Rashi's Commentary,* vol. 2, *Shemoth* (Jerusalem: Silbermann Family, 1934), 121 b.

9. Levenson, *The Death and Resurrection of the Beloved Son,* 11-12, 36.

This ideal lies at the deepest level of Jewish spirituality. It undergirds the stories that ground Israel's conviction that its very existence as God's special people depends on the offering of Isaac by Abraham, of Benjamin by Jacob/Israel, and then of the Passover lamb in the land of Egypt, which exempted Israel's own firstborn from dying along with those of the Egyptians. Indeed, as the text makes clear, the Exodus itself is a matter of the liberation not merely of an oppressed people, but of God's *firstborn son* to go and serve the God *to whom that son belongs:* "Then you shall say to Pharaoh, 'Thus says the LORD: Israel is my first-born son. I have said to you, "Let My son go, that he may worship Me," yet you refuse to let him go. Hence, I will slay your first-born son'" (Exodus 4:21-23, JPS). The Exodus story has nothing to do with an opposition to slavery, an idea found neither in the Hebrew Bible nor in the New Testament.[10] The weight lies rather just where it does in the *aqedah,* in the mystery of God's special relationship to a beloved son conceived despite human infertility by the inscrutable will of *Hashem.*

It is clear that Jeremiah and Ezekiel wanted to abolish not only the practice but the very idea of child sacrifice. If they had had their way, the story of the binding of Isaac might well have been excised from the First Book of Moses. In fact, however, the idea never died out. It was transformed instead.[11]

The story of the binding of Isaac has a most strange history. It lay dormant during the whole biblical period and is not even mentioned or referred to in the rest of the Hebrew scriptures (with the indirect, postexilic exception of 2 Chronicles 3:1). Then, in the postbiblical period, especially during the time of the Roman occupation, it stimulated a new exegetical tradition that transformed the story and made it central. Instead of stressing the faithful obedience of Abraham, however, the story was retold with increasing

---

10. Levenson, *The Death and Resurrection of the Beloved Son,* 37.
11. Hence the subtitle of Levenson's book: *The Transformation of Child Sacrifice in Judaism and Christianity.*

emphasis on Isaac and his readiness, his willingness, even his joyful eagerness, to throw himself on the altar for the sake of his descendants. By the first century C.E. the change was incorporated in the tradition[12]

In the retold story, moreover, Isaac's joyful self-sacrifice was thought to have taken place in some sense. In a text that was probably written somewhere "around the time of Jesus,"[13] we hear of Isaac's blood and then of his being "given back" by God.[14] Already the development into a story of an atoning death, with Isaac reduced to ashes, followed by his resurrection from the dead, was under way.[15]

This retelling of the *aqedah* did not take place in a historical vacuum. The development seems to have occurred in the period after the Maccabean revolt, when Jews needed a theology of martyrdom to account for the death of their bravest and best sons. Isaac became the model for all future martyrs, giving his life for the sake of his descendants. According to 4 Maccabees 13:12, a document written somewhere between about 18 and 55 C.E.,[16] one of the martyrs, addressing his brothers, appealed to the retold *aqedah*: "Remember whence you came and at the hand of what father Isaac gave himself to be sacrificed for piety's sake."

This development was based on a growing tendency to read all of Israel's history in the light of the story of Abraham, including

12. Geza Vermes, *Scripture and Tradition in Judaism* (Leiden: Brill, 1961), 204. In this essay, entitled "Redemption and Genesis xxii — The Binding of Isaac and the Sacrifice of Christ," Vermes published, if in much briefer compass, the core of what Levenson has more recently brought to our attention.

13. D. J. Harrington, "Pseudo-Philo," in *The Old Testament Pseudepigrapha*, 2 vols., ed. James H. Charlesworth (New York: Doubleday, 1983-85), 2:299.

14. Pseudo-Philo, *Biblical Antiquities* 18:5, in *The Old Testament Pseudepigrapha*, ed. Charlesworth, 2:325.

15. Levenson, *The Death and Resurrection of the Beloved Son*, 198-99. For the further development, see Spiegel, *The Last Trial*.

16. See H. Anderson, "4 Maccabees," in *The Old Testament Pseudepigrapha*, ed. Charlesworth, 2:534.

the *aqedah*. This exegetical tradition laid stress on the expectation that God acted measure for measure toward Israel in response to Abraham's and Isaac's righteous actions, splitting the sea for Isaac's descendants as Abraham had split the wood for the sacrifice of Isaac. Since Abraham and Isaac were willing to make this sacrifice for their descendants, God would remember it and act to redeem his people.

The principle of measure for measure,[17] coupled with the association of the Maccabean martyrs with Isaac, also accounts for another phrase in 4 Maccabees (17:21), which calls their deaths "a ransom for the sin of our nation, as it were." The affirmation of the next verse is even more striking (17:22): "Through the blood of these righteous ones and through the propitiation of their death the divine providence rescued Israel . . ." In Romans 3:25 Paul used the same word — *hilastērion,* "propitiation" — with reference to Christ's death.

Modern discussion over the past century and a quarter of the relationship of the *aqedah* to the New Testament has been distorted by the apologetic hostility of both Jewish and Christian scholars. The anger seems to arise at the least suggestion that one's own tradition has borrowed and learned something from the other. In an extensive and remarkably nonapologetic review of this discussion, James Swetnam focuses primarily on the influence of the *aqedah* tradition on the Epistle to the Hebrews, not on 1 Corinthians 15.[18] The emphasis in that tradition on Isaac's joy is echoed in Hebrews 12:2 (". . . Jesus . . . who for the joy that was set before him endured the cross . . .") and in Hebrews 9:14 ("offered himself without blemish to God"). The sublimation of Isaac's sacrifice in self-sacrifice is also at work in John 10:17-18: "I lay down my life that I may take it again. No one takes it from me, but I lay it down of my own accord."

17. Burton L. Visotzky, *Reading the Book: Making the Bible a Timeless Text* (New York: Doubleday, 1991), 125-40, gives many examples of the use of the idea of measure for measure.

18. James Swetnam, *Jesus and Isaac: A Study of the Epistle to the Hebrews in the Light of the Aqedah* (Rome: Pontifical Biblical Institute, 1981).

I grant to Raymond Brown that there is no "certitude" about the influence of the *aqedah*.[19] Yet the language of the primitive gospel seems very much at home in the interpretive world of the Jewish literature in which the *aqedah* was developing. Apart from this world, the language of the gospel is enigmatic, and I prefer a plausible hypothesis to none at all. The hypothesis, again, is that our early, pre-Pauline gospel was the result of a highly creative application of the early Jewish interpretation of the binding of Isaac to the crucifixion of Jesus and to the events (or discovery) occurring perhaps on the first day of the next week, so as to turn those days into Good Friday and Easter.

This use of the binding of Isaac entails an unsettling implication that cannot be glossed over.[20] If Jesus is seen to have taken up the role of Isaac, then God must have taken over Abraham's role. But if God offered up his beloved son, to whom was the offering made? The question has no answer, perhaps because it is irrelevant. What matters is that the principle of "measure for measure" has been radicalized — one might say extended to the breaking point — both by Paul in Romans 8:32 ("He who did not spare his own Son but gave him up for us all . . .") and by the author of John 3:16 ("God so loved the world that he gave his only Son"). The extension, although radical, is itself a reminder of the exegetical context and character of the discovery of the early gospel.

What objections are there to this hypothesis? One is that Isaac is not mentioned in the pre-Pauline gospel, nor is Jesus identified as the new Isaac. Indeed, Isaac is not mentioned at all. My response is that the four Gospels do not call Jesus "Israel" or "the new Israel,"

---

19. Raymond E. Brown, "Appendix VI: The Sacrifice of Isaac and the Passion," in *The Death of the Messiah* (New York: Doubleday, 1994), 2:1435-44. Brown's skeptical conclusion is based on a less extensive review of the texts than Swetnam's, and he focuses on the passion narratives, rather than on the primitive gospel.

20. This has been noted by both Nils Alstrup Dahl, *Jesus the Christ: The Historical Origins of Christological Doctrine,* ed. Donald H. Juel (Minneapolis: Fortress, 1991), 142, and Levenson, *The Death and Resurrection of the Beloved Son,* 223.

yet, as will be discussed in Chapter 6, they tell the life of Jesus as the story of Israel. It could be further objected that our account of the evolution of first-century interpretation of scripture has ignored the characteristically Jewish methods of exegesis discussed in the last chapter. Perhaps there is no contradiction, however. The phrase "son of David," who was already called God's son in the messianic Psalms, could have led to texts dealing with the son who is archetypal for the whole postbiblical tradition of Israel, Abraham's son Isaac. Once this had occurred, the words "only son" and "beloved" could have led the exegete also to the stories of Joseph and Benjamin, beloved sons given up and restored. Such a process might have formed a part of the discovery of the early gospel, and it would also explain how, when the evangelists wanted to tell the story of Jesus, they told it in the form of a story of the death and resurrection of the beloved son, fittingly opened with a voice from heaven saying "This is my beloved son" and written by authors who knew what lay in wait for a beloved son.

If our hypothesis is sound, then we can say that the church's faith and identity are grounded in the same story as is the faith and identity of the Jewish people. The two communities are bound together by the binding of Isaac. That is a remarkable bond, but it puts us in something of a bind, for those Jews who believed Jesus to have been the new Isaac for the whole world parted company from those Jews who did not. This might not necessarily have been a bad thing. They might have said that their gospel was from God, revealed to Peter and the Twelve, and then passed on to Paul, by way of the Jewish exegetical tradition of the *aqedah*. Unhappily, they and (even more so) the Gentiles whom they welcomed into their company came to regard those other Jews as their enemies, even as enemies of God. Then, as they developed their story of the death and resurrection of the beloved son, they portrayed those other Jews as enemies of Jesus and responsible for his death, in spite of the fact that he died on a Roman cross. This set the church on a course of Christian anti-Judaism that prepared the way for modern anti-Semitism.

Must it continue today? Can Christians stand by their central *mythos* of Christ as the new Isaac for the whole world and yet affirm the Jewish people as God's chosen and firstborn son? A few Christians began wrestling with this question some fifty years ago, and as time has passed many more have joined in this rethinking. But the task is difficult: patterns of thought and practice that endured from the first and second centuries until the middle of the twentieth century do not change easily. Nevertheless, as the church was born out of a highly creative application of a most highly creative development of the *aqedah,* so Christians today are called to an equally creative reinterpretation of their tradition.

CHAPTER 5

The Gospel and Paul

THERE CAN BE LITTLE DOUBT that what Paul termed his calling, or what the church has called his conversion, marked a dramatic turn in his life. Insofar as Paul writes of it (e.g., in Galatians 1:15), he uses the language with which some of Israel's prophets speak of their calling (cf. Isaiah 49:1, 5, and especially Jeremiah 1:5). He saw it as a new, prophetic calling within the continuing story of Israel, not as a turn to a new religion, a concept Paul would not have understood.[1] This calling, however, turned his life around and caused him to count as secondary to it all that he had known and loved before.

Paul speaks in Galatians 1:16, referring perhaps to this same experience, of God's revelation of his Son to him. But every revelation reaches human beings in a human way. As Rabbi Joshua said of the Torah, "It is not in the heavens," and as the Talmud says repeatedly, "Torah speaks in the language of human beings."[2] If the recipient of a revelation speaks of it, he or she will be using human words. Paul preached his gospel in words. Had Paul first heard those

---

1. On this, see Krister Stendahl, *Paul Among Jews and Gentiles and Other Essays* (Philadelphia: Fortress, 1976), 7-23.

2. *Baba Meṣi'a* 59b. I learned the Talmud saying from Rabbi David Hartman.

words from God, say, in his imagination? As G. B. Shaw's Joan of Arc puts it, when a skeptic says that the "voices" which she says come from God come in fact from her imagination: "Of course. That is how the messages of God come to us."[3]

An alternative source is suggested, however, by Paul's statement in Philippians 3:5 that he was trained as a Pharisee. As such he was aware of their teaching that the tradition of oral interpretation of the Torah, what he called "the traditions of my fathers " (Gal. 1:14), had been revealed by God. This tradition was soon to be called the "oral Torah" and came to be regarded as surely from heaven as the written Torah, the first five books of the scriptures, given by God to Moses at Sinai. In any case, Paul believed that God had made it possible that human words might become the word of God.

The merit of reading Galatians 1:11-12 in the light of 1 Corinthians 15:3, as we did in Chapter 1, is that an investigation of the origin of the gospel remains in the realm of human words, with no need to deny their potential status as revelation. It therefore sets us on the path to asking about Paul and the gospel that he received, and what he contributed to it.

Another formulation of the gospel that Paul learned is found in the opening of his letter to the Romans (1:3-4). Paul introduces it as "God's gospel — which he promised long ago through his prophets in the sacred scriptures, concerning his Son . . ." I shall follow a recent commentator on this epistle, Joseph A. Fitzmyer, in putting in italics the words which he and others believe, on stylistic and linguistic grounds, to be Paul's own words rather than a received formulation:

> . . . his Son, born of David's stock, according to the flesh, established
> as Son of God *with power,* according to a spirit of holiness *as of the
> resurrection from the dead,* Jesus Christ our Lord.[4]

3. This exchange occurs in Scene One of Shaw's play *Saint Joan.*
4. See Joseph A. Fitzmyer, *Romans: A New Translation with Introduction and Commentary,* Anchor Bible, vol. 33 (New York: Doubleday, 1993), 229-37, for arguments for and against Pauline authorship of each phrase. I follow his translation, 227.

The crucial themes are familiar: Jesus Christ is the subject, and he is God's Son. He is by birth the seed of David, a designation not elsewhere occurring in Paul's authentic letters, and, by a Spirit of holiness (a Semitism), the Son of God. If "with power" was not part of the formulation, it implies that before his resurrection Jesus was Son of God in weakness. Since his resurrection, he is God's Son either by God's great act, or more likely, as a source of power.[5] The resurrection was evidently not specified in the formulation, Christ's exaltation, or, more accurately, his vindication, being expressed as his establishment as Son of God by a Spirit of holiness. Did its formulators not know that others were using "resurrection"? Paul, apparently considering the two versions to be mutually consistent, felt free to cite the one, "established as Son of God according to a Spirit of holiness," and also to add the other, "as of his resurrection from the dead."

Further, there is no mention of the cross or even of Jesus' death. It seems that this other formulation does not merely say less than that of 1 Corinthians 15; it was an assessment of Jesus without the recitation of a narrative of the end of his life. On the other hand, in speaking of him as of the seed of David and Son of God, this too was a gospel according to the scriptures, as Paul's introduction says. On the whole, however, Romans seems to reflect an early interpretation of Jesus different in important respects from the one that is at the center of our investigation. This should remind us that even if my hypothesis is correct, it does not exhaust the diversity of the beginnings of Christianity.

As was mentioned in Chapter 1, there is yet another passage in Paul's letters that scholars are inclined to take as being pre-Pauline,[6] in which there is less consensus on the extent of its Pauline editing: Philippians 2:5-11. This hymnic form of the gospel reads:

---

5. See Fitzmyer, *Romans,* 235 and the literature cited there.

6. See Alan F. Segal, *Paul the Convert: The Apostolate and Apostasy of Saul the Pharisee* (New Haven and London: Yale University Press, 1990), 62 and the literature cited in the notes.

. . . Christ Jesus,
who, though he was in the form of God,
   did not count equality with God a thing to be grasped,
but emptied himself, taking the form of a slave,
   being born in the likeness of men.
And being found in human form he humbled himself
   and became obedient unto death, even death on a cross.
Therefore God has highly exalted him
   and bestowed on him the name which is above every name,
that at the name of Jesus every knee should bow,
   in heaven and on earth and under the earth,
and every tongue confess that Jesus Christ is Lord,
   to the glory of God the Father.

   ·   The echoes of scripture[7] are strong: the wording of the phrase "in the form of God" is different from what Genesis 1:26 says of *'ādām,* "in our image, after our likeness," but the thought seems to be echoed. Christ as the second Adam was not an unknown concept to the early movement (1 Corinthians 15:45; Romans 5:14). Further, the phrase "equality with God" echoes the serpent's words of Genesis 3:5: "you will be like God," and the phrase "taking the form of a slave" recalls Pharaoh's slave, Israel (Deuteronomy 6:21), more probably than it might the servant of *Hashem* of Isaiah 49 and 53, since this figure has apparently not yet crystallized in first-century Jewish thought.[8] Humiliation and exaltation are, of course, the central themes, as they are in the version of 1 Corinthians. On Jesus is "bestowed the name" of God himself, as it was on Israel, which is called by God's name (Isaiah 43:7; Jeremiah 14:9). Just as

---

7. See Richard B. Hays, *Echoes of Scripture in the Letters of Paul* (New Haven and London: Yale University Press, 1989), 18-21, who makes use of the concept and theory of echoes in John Hollander, *The Figure of Echo: A Mode of Allusion in Milton and After* (Berkeley: University of California Press, 1981). Hays does not discuss Philippians 2:5-11 or its echoes of scripture.

8. Donald Juel, *Messianic Exegesis: Christological Interpretation of the Old Testament in Early Christianity* (Philadelphia: Fortress, 1988), 127.

his humiliation (actively accepted, as in the contemporary interpretations of the *aqedah*) was without limit, so is his exaltation.
Finally, the words of Isaiah 45:23 echo clearly in "every knee should
bow" and "every tongue confess."[9] This hymn, too, is a gospel
according to the scriptures and to their postbiblical Jewish interpretation, even while it goes beyond that interpretation.

Unlike the version of the early gospel rehearsed in Romans 1,
this one is most explicit about Jesus' death on a cross, far more than
the version of 1 Corinthians 15. God's vindication of Jesus, however,
is not interpreted by means of a resurrection, but with the concept
of exaltation. To this I add that the tradition of an empty tomb has
left no mark on any of the three, 1 Corinthians 15:3-4, Romans
1:3-4, or Philippians 2:5-11, perhaps because the tradition had not
yet been developed.

The differences among the three formulations of the pre-Pauline gospel tempt us to order them in a chronological sequence,
perhaps with the simplest form as the earliest (Romans 1), followed
by 1 Corinthians, with Philippians 2, the most developed, coming
last. But this linear development is pure conjecture. It is equally if
not more likely that these are versions of the primitive gospel formulated in different communities of the Jesus movement.[10] The
differences are obvious, especially those of Romans 1 from the other
two, but so are the agreements. In all three cases, the gospel is an
interpretation of Jesus as the beloved Son of God, clearly derived
from the scriptures of Israel as interpreted by first-century Jews. If
an interpretation of the events of Jesus' end as the death and resurrection of Jesus Christ is at most only implicit in Romans, in
Philippians these events are presented as the humiliation of crucifi-

---

9. "This passage is modelled on Isaiah xlv.23" (J. B. Lightfoot, *St. Paul's Epistle
to the Philippians* [London: Macmillan, 1890]), 114.

10. Burton L. Mack, *A Myth of Innocence: Mark and Christian Origins* (Philadelphia: Fortress, 1988), would say that these were gospels of the Christ cult, rather than
of the Jesus movement. The gospel of Romans 1, however, mentions neither the death
nor the resurrection of Jesus, presumed marks of the Christ cult's myth.

xion, followed (or rewarded) by exaltation. The three versions may be seen as examples of the diverse ways in which the scriptures and the Jewish traditions were applied to Jesus by his Jewish followers.

What then was Paul's contribution? Did he add anything to the gospel he received? The most striking move, which clearly goes beyond contemporary Jewish exegesis, comes in his use of the language of the *aqedah* in Romans 8:32: "He who did not spare his own Son but gave him up for us all, will he not give us all things with him?" This was a move in line with a contemporary trend in Jewish reading of the *aqedah,* which was stressing, on the principle of measure for measure, that God could be expected to act toward Israel in a manner corresponding to Abraham's act of faithful obedience. Nils Dahl's striking comment warrants citing:

> Yet at the crucial point — Abraham's offering of his son — the principle was not applied in non-Christian Judaism. Only an interpreter who believed the crucified Jesus to be Messiah and Son of God could dare to follow the trend to its bitter end, saying that as Abraham offered up his son, so God offered up his own Son for Isaac's children.[11]

It has often been said that Paul's major contribution to the Christian movement was his concept of the atonement, or more specifically, his concept of Christ's vicarious sacrificial death. Fitzmyer, for example, in defense of Paul's originality on this point, claims that no postbiblical Jewish source interprets Genesis 22 as a vicarious sacrifice: "that Isaac was to be sacrificed on behalf of Israel, or on behalf of anyone else, is never mentioned."[12]

In fact, however, Genesis 22:16-17 says explicitly that Abraham will be blessed precisely because he was willing to offer up his son

---

11. Nils Alstrup Dahl, *Jesus the Christ: The Historical Origins of Christological Doctrine,* ed. Donald H. Juel (Minneapolis: Fortress, 1991), 142.

12. Fitzmyer, *Romans,* 531. He refers to *4 Maccabees* 7:14; 13:12; 16:20; 18:11; *Jubilees* 17:15, 18, 19; and to Josephus, Philo, and Pseudo-Philo.

Isaac. Pseudo-Philo, as we have seen, developed that connection when he has God say of Isaac: "On account of his blood, I chose them [Israel]."[13] Again, the author of 4 Maccabees has one of the martyrs encourage his companions with the words "Remember whence you came and at the hand of what father Isaac gave himself to be sacrificed for piety's sake" (13:12), and writes of the Maccabean martyrs: "They became, as it were, a ransom for the sin of our nation. Through the blood of these righteous ones and through the propitiation of their death the divine providence rescued Israel" (17:21, 22). As we have noted, the Greek word *hilastērion,* "propitiation," from the term (Exodus 25:17-22 in the Septuagint) for the covering of the ark and the place from which God spoke to Moses, is the same word Paul used in Romans 3:25 referring to Christ Jesus: "whom God put forward as a propitiation by his blood."

Let it be said that neither in the case of the Maccabean martyrs nor in that of Christ is there the faintest idea that a human death can or ought to appease an angry god. This idea may be found in other religious traditions, but it is distinguished by its absence from both the Jewish and the Christian traditions. If Israel had a practice of sacrifices offered in the Temple, that was because Israel's God had graciously provided and ordered this way for Israel to present its life, Israel's sin as well as its accomplishments, before God. If a death effects a reconciliation, this occurs because God has chosen to regard it in this way. Propitiation is a divinely instituted means of reconciliation provided by the love of God.

Jon Levenson and Geza Vermes before him have called our attention to these postbiblical sources to show "that Isaac was to be

13. Pseudo-Philo, *Biblical Antiquities* 18:5; translation by D. J. Harrington, "Pseudo-Philo," in *The Old Testament Pseudepigrapha,* 2 vols., ed. James H. Charlesworth (New York: Doubleday, 1983-85), 2:325. The following citations from *4 Maccabees* are from H. Anderson, "4 Maccabees," in *The Old Testament Pseudepigrapha,* ed. Charlesworth, 2:558, 563. Cf. Jon D. Levenson, *The Death and Resurrection of the Beloved Son: The Transformation of Child Sacrifice in Judaism and Christianity* (New Haven and London: Yale University Press, 1993), 187-88.

sacrificed on behalf of Israel." Given Fitzmyer's contradictory claim, we are forced to choose between these interpretations of postbiblical Jewish texts. I suggest that we follow the advice of Ignatius, the early second-century bishop of Antioch, in his letter to the church in Philadelphia: "It is better to hear Christianity from the circumcised than Judaism from the uncircumcised."[14] The conclusion from the available evidence is that the idea of vicarious sacrifice was not an original Pauline contribution to the gospel that he received.

In considering the origin of the idea of vicarious sacrifice, it will help Christians avoid a possible self-defensive apologetic if they remember that it is most unlikely that any of the writers we are discussing would have thought of themselves as anything other than Jewish. It must be pointed out, further, that a thought or idea does not have to be original in order to be from God. To assume or assert that there can be no revelation in a borrowed idea presupposes a god who can reveal himself only in an external intervention and never through the interaction of human beings. On the contrary, the church has always insisted that God's word has come through the human witness of Israel. Christians can welcome this teaching as the church's recognition that it has been allowed to share in Israel's story.

It appears, therefore, that although Paul only explicitly ac-knowledged having received one of the formulations of the gospel he taught, his letters reveal that he knew it in several versions, all of which may have originated with the beginning of the movement. On the human level, that gospel could be called an exegetical discovery, but it was more basically a daring application to Jesus, and to the events of his end, of the radical discovery evident in parts of postbiblical Jewish exegesis or midrash: the transformation of the *aqedah* into the story of the death and resurrection of the beloved son. It may have been Peter, listed as the first to whom the risen Christ appeared, who, in searching the scriptures for understanding,

14. Ignatius, *Letter to the Philadelphians* 6:1.

first made the application. In this he was followed by "the Twelve," and among them there may well have been more than one version of what they had discovered. Last of all, it was Paul's discovery, probably also in searching the scriptures (could it have been Isaiah 49 that he studied?) in Damascus,[15] however much influenced he may have been by believers in the gospel that he first abhorred and then embraced.

Paul's special contribution lies less in Christology or in any theory of the atonement than in his insistence that this gospel be preached to Gentiles as well as to Jews. He believed that God had called him for this purpose (Galatians 1:16), and that this too was according to the scriptures. So he was understood by the authors of the epistles to the Colossians and to the Ephesians, who, speaking in Paul's name, wrote: "the mystery was made known to me by revelation . . . how the Gentiles are fellow heirs" (Ephesians 3:3, 6) and again, "the mystery hidden for ages and generations but now made manifest to his saints. To them God chose to make known how great among the Gentiles are the riches of the glory of this mystery" (Colossians 1:26-27). The gospel that Paul preached to the Gentiles, however new it may have been for them, and however unprecedented for them the consequences, was nevertheless the gospel that Paul himself had received of the self-offered death for us and the resurrection of God's Son, all of it according to the Jewish scriptures.

15. Paul's sketchy account in Galatians 1:17 implies that his revelation occurred in Damascus. "On the road to Damascus" appears to be an invention of the author of Acts, writing some two to three generations after the event.

CHAPTER 6

The Gospel and the Gospels

NEAR THE TIME OF or shortly after the fall of Jerusalem and the destruction of the Temple (70 C.E.), one of the young Christian communities produced something new: the Gospel according to Mark. In the following decades, other communities produced the Gospels according to Matthew, Luke, and John. These Gospels were compositions built out of the gospel that Paul received and also, woven together with it, what may be called the Jesus tradition or traditions. These traditions were derived partly from what Jesus' Galilean disciples, or the communities stemming from different groups of disciples, presumably remembered of what he had said and done, and partly from the teachings of the individual communities. The Gospels, I shall argue, resulted from setting these traditions within the controlling framework of the pre-Pauline gospel.

The Gospels are clearly different from the early gospel. Mark fashioned a narrative not simply of Jesus' end, but of the whole way of the one who ended by being crucified as "King of the Jews" and proclaimed as the crucified Messiah, raised and exalted by God. Mark, whose Gospel I am assuming (with most scholars) to have been the earliest, began his narrative of Jesus' way with the story of his baptism as the beginning of his public career, opening with the words "The beginning of the gospel of Jesus Christ, the Son of God," followed by a verse from Malachi and one from Isaiah (both attributed to Isaiah), and then the story of Jesus' baptism by John. Matthew and Luke pushed the beginning of the story back to Jesus' birth, complete with genealogies going back to Abraham or even to Adam. The author of the Fourth Gospel pushed it back to his existence with God "in the beginning." All of them end with his death on a cross and versions of the new beginning of Easter, these being clearly presented as the goal of his way and the climax of his story. The Gospels have the effect, therefore, of underscoring that this gospel is about Jesus of Nazareth by telling his story as the one to whom all this happened. He is its protagonist, even if its hidden subject, revealed only through the totality of the narrative, is God.

The Gospels, moreover, do more than simply include an account of Jesus' ministry as a preface to the story of his end. As Howard Kee has pointed out, the well-known characterization of the Gospels by Martin Kähler as "passion narratives with extended introductions" is not adequate.[1] Even Helmut Köster's modification, that the Gospel of Mark is "nothing but a passion narrative with a biographical introduction," fails to do justice to the fact that the so-called introduction makes up five-sixths of Mark's Gospel, by Kee's count.[2] The Galilean tradition (or traditions) concerning Jesus, and so the story of his whole life, was evidently important for the community that produced the Gospel according to Mark. And we may recall that whenever Paul had access to that tradition, he called upon it as having binding halakic authority for the communities that he founded.

On the other hand, the difference between the Gospels and

---

1. Howard Clark Kee, *Community of the New Age: Studies in Mark's Gospel* (Philadelphia: Westminster, 1977), 30. The characterization by Kähler was made in his influential *Der sogenannte historische Jesus und der geschichtliche, biblische Christus* (Leipzig: Deichert, 1892), a protest against the Life-of-Jesus research in the nineteenth century.

2. Kee, *Community of the New Age,* 31.

the gospel should not be exaggerated, for the former are dependent on the latter. As Donald Juel comments in his interpretation of Mark, "the origin of Mark's Christology is to be sought in the history of Jesus of Nazareth," but he then adds, "principally in the events that brought his career to an end and offered a whole new beginning. . . . While other aspects of Jesus' history have shaped the narrative, . . . none has had as decisive an impact on the shape of the narrative as the death of the would-be king."[3] Or, as James Dunn has put it, "from the beginning Christianity's claims regarding Jesus have always been about the whole Christ-event, particularly his death and resurrection, and never simply his life as though that had independent value distinct from his passion and exaltation."[4] What the Gospels tell is the story of that "whole Christ-event," and they tell it throughout as leading up to that passion and exaltation, apart from which their narrative would have had for them no particular value. That is to say, the gospel comes first; then comes the narrative of him who is its center. In short, the gospel determined the narrative; the gospel was developed into the Gospels.

It may be a modern discovery that Jesus of Nazareth, insofar as he is recoverable by critical historians, fits so well into his first-century Galilean Jewish environment that he appears to have had little to say that was distinctively his own. The discovery, however, is one that the evangelists, if they could have understood the interest of modern historians, would not have found surprising. What made Jesus of Nazareth and his teaching distinctive and important for them was that he was the crucified and raised Messiah. Mark's narrative was, as he said, "the gospel of Jesus Christ, the Son of God."

In addition, the Gospels share a crucial feature with the gospel:

3. Donald Juel, *A Master of Surprise: Mark Interpreted* (Minneapolis: Fortress, 1994), 104.
4. James D. G. Dunn, *Christology in the Making: A New Testament Inquiry into the Origins of the Doctrine of the Incarnation*, 2d ed. (Grand Rapids: Eerdmans, 1996), 254.

they too are through and through "according to the scriptures." Not only does Mark introduce those prophetic verses that interpret the tradition that Jesus began his public career as a disciple of John the Baptist, but the baptism narrative concludes with the freighted words from heaven, using the language and a crucial theme of the scriptures, "an appropriate source of language," as Juel remarks, "for a voice from heaven": "This is my beloved Son; with you I am well pleased." The words are from Psalm 2:7 and Isaiah 42:1, and more crucial is the echo of Genesis 22:2, the opening of the story of the binding of the beloved son Isaac.

Psalm 22 provided much of the narrative detail for the passion narrative, but the larger narrative of Jesus' life is modeled on Israel's story. Mark's Gospel ends, as we have noticed, with the disciples speechless under the impact of the empty tomb.[5] The Gospel itself, however, is evident testimony to the fact that the disciples were rescued from their speechlessness. If we attend to the words which Mark used, we can see that they found their way out of their speechlessness with the help of the scriptures of their Jewish tradition. There they found the words with which to speak of the death and resurrection of Jesus. So it came about that he died for us and was raised always "according to the scriptures," and often word for word. Was he in fact born in Bethlehem? (See Micah 5:1 [JPS]: "O Bethlehem . . . , from you shall come forth to rule Israel for Me one whose origin is from of old.") Did Judas in fact receive thirty pieces of silver to betray him? (See Zechariah 11:12 [JPS]: "So they weighed out my wages, thirty shekels of silver.") Was Jesus actually crucified between criminals and buried in a rich man's tomb? (See Isaiah 53:9: "And they made his grave with the wicked, and with a rich man in his death.") Did Roman soldiers really cast lots for his garments? (See Psalm 22:18: "They divided my gar-

5. The whole of this paragraph is indebted especially to Friedrich-Wilhelm Marquardt, *Das christliche Bekenntnis zu Jesus, dem Juden,* 2 vols. (Munich: Kaiser, 1990-91).

ments among them, and for my raiment they cast lots.") I doubt we shall ever know. What we can surely know is that all these and many other details were told of him in words taken from the scriptures. The result is that Jesus — the only Jesus whom the church or anyone else has ever known — meets us and comes to us clothed in and inseparable from the scriptures of his people. The Christian community cannot have and never has had either one without the other.

This intimate relationship between Jesus and the scriptures is also underscored in other ways. Some of the Gospels recount the life of Jesus as the story of one who relived the life and history of his people, going down to and returning from Egypt as a child (Matthew), with forty days in the wilderness recapitulating the forty years of Israelite wilderness wandering before entering the land of promise (Mark, Matthew, and Luke). Again, according to the end of Luke's Gospel (24:27), the risen Jesus stirred up his disciples' imagination to see Israel's scriptures as witnessing to him: "And beginning with Moses and all the prophets, he interpreted to them in all the scriptures the things concerning himself." The scriptures never existed for the disciples or the later church apart from that interpretation, and so firm was this connection that it continued to determine Christian readings of the scriptures beyond that of the first generation. Thus no Christian, at least since the second century, has ever been able to read the so-called servant-poems of Isaiah — for example that in chapter 53 — without immediately thinking of Jesus:

> He was despised, shunned by men,
>> A man of suffering, familiar with disease. . . .
> Yet it was our sickness that he was bearing,
>> Our suffering that he endured.
> We accounted him plagued,
>> Smitten and afflicted by God;
> But he was wounded because of our sins,
>> Crushed because of our iniquities.

> He bore the chastisement that made us whole,
> And by his bruises we were healed. (Isaiah 53:3a, 4-5, JPS)

To what extent the disciples told the story of Jesus in the light and language of the scriptures, and to what extent Jesus first lived his life in conformity with those scriptures, is not possible for us to sort out, since the evidence for both views is the same. Nor do I think it necessary for any Christian to decide, for either way we are only saying that in the Gospels, and so for the critical historian of the Christian tradition as well as for the believing Christian, Jesus is available only as he comes wrapped in Israel's scriptures, and those scriptures, as sacred scriptures for the Christian community, exist and can only exist for that community as bearing witness to the Jew from Nazareth. It is therefore misleading to say that the church finds Jesus in the scriptures, the so-called Old Testament. What it finds is that the scriptures speak of Jesus, because it was from Israel's scriptures that it first learned how to speak of him. It learned from the first to speak of him in Israel's idiom.[6] For this reason, we may say that Israel's scriptures are foundational for the Gospels as well as for the gospel that Paul received. Without those scriptures and the conviction of the disciples that reality was to be found therein, there would have been no gospel, and so no church and no Gospels.

Over the past two hundred years, there have been many who have tried to build their faith on Jesus apart from those scriptures. He has been portrayed as everything from a religious genius to a freedom fighter, from a moral philosopher to a revolutionary. All too often he has been made into an anti-Judaic Jesus. Compared to some of these pictures, the more recent ones of "Jesus the Jew"[7] at least have the merit of associating him positively with his own people. The church has survived, more or less, with all of these pictures, but in most cases, they are a series of attempts to have a Jesus according to the New

6. Marquardt, *Das christliche Bekenntnis,* esp. 1:140ff.
7. Discussed in Chapter 1 above.

Testament. The result, of course, is inevitably a secondhand Jesus, for the authors of the New Testament itself formed their various pictures of Jesus "according to the scriptures."

The church's reflection on its deepest convictions is impoverished when it fails to read the New Testament in the light of the Old Testament. This can be illustrated by reference to a common reading of the classic text for the doctrine of the incarnation, John 1:14. This is usually read without attention to the parallelism so characteristic of the scriptures and noticed by most Christians only in the Psalms.[8] So John 1:14 is read, "And the word became flesh." That, however, is but the first half of a two-part sentence, omitting the parallel, "and pitched his tent among us" (my translation). In scriptural parallelism, the second half of a verse is no mere subordinate commentary on the first half but is constructed to say the same thing in other words. The other words, in this case, call to mind the tent of meeting described in the book of Exodus (33:7-11), the tabernacle of God among his people Israel. The parallel should lead us to see that the Johannine story of the incarnation of the Word in Jesus is to be read in conjunction with the story of God's presence with his people in the tent of meeting, where "the LORD used to speak to Moses face to face, as a man speaks to his friend" (Exodus 33:11; it is precisely in the Gospel according to John that Jesus calls his disciples "friends," 15:13-15). To ignore so explicit a reference to the scriptures is to miss an essential part of the message not only of those who first discovered the pre-Pauline gospel, but also of those who produced the Gospels. We thereby fail to see that the "highest" christological themes and confessions were themselves discovered and formulated "according to the scriptures."

To read the Gospels as windows through which we may glimpse reality is to use them for a purpose for which they were never intended. When so read, they may be taken as the surviving evidence of the traces of a "real" Jesus, but a Jesus unknown to their authors. Read

8. Marquardt, *Das christliche Bekenntnis*, 2:111-16.

with appreciation for the understanding of those who produced them and of those for whom they were composed originally, not to speak of the Christian tradition (at least until modern times), they become the gospel in narrative form, the story of the crucified and risen Messiah. In the one case, we are led to seek a Jesus behind the text; in the other, we may find the Jesus of the text, and so not simply the "Jesus of the New Testament," but the Jesus according to the scriptures, who is historically the real Jesus of the New Testament.

Should we take sides over this? It depends on what we wish to find. If we seek the Jesus of history, which is the Jesus constructed, necessarily hypothetically, by the methods of modern historiography, then we shall find such a Jesus, viewed as he perhaps may have been seen by those of his contemporaries who did not know or were not interested in the way in which his death and Easter were seen by those of his followers who produced the gospel. It is fairly evident, however, that such a Jesus, whatever connection he may have had to the Jesus of those movements that produced the various traditions behind "Q" and the Gospel of Thomas, is not the one whose death and resurrection were celebrated by those Jews who turned out to be the founders of the church. It was not "the historical Jesus" who turned those Jews into believers in "Jesus Christ, the Son of God" (so both the beginning of the earliest Gospel, Mark 1:1, and the original ending of the last Gospel, John 20:31). For the Jesus of the Gospels, like the Jesus of the gospel, is Jesus "according to the scriptures," and this is the one in whom the church trusted in the beginning and in whom it claims to trust to this day.

These reflections on the relationship between the gospel and the Gospels lead to a conclusion that may be stated briefly. The Gospels did not arise as a result of simply adding the gospel to the tradition concerning Jesus of Nazareth, but as a result of interpreting and revising that tradition in the light of the already existing gospel "according to the scriptures." Consequently, that tradition came to be likewise built up out of, filtered through, and interpreted "according to the scriptures."

PART II

THE SCRIPTURES
OF THE GOSPEL

CHAPTER 7

So What about the Scriptures?

THE DISCOVERY OF THE GOSPEL according to the scriptures was at the same time the discovery of the Old Testament. Less compactly expressed, in discovering the gospel according to the scriptures, the disciples discovered a new reading of Israel's scriptures that turned them into the context, the foundations, and the source of the actual vocabulary of that gospel. Israel's scriptures interpreted in this way became the foundation of the early church. They became the church's Bible, and, when the writings that make up the New Testament were added, they became the church's Old Testament.

It has been said that Christianity is the only world religion born with its Bible in its cradle. This is only superficially true, for its Bible was not simply the inherited Jewish scriptures, but those scriptures interpreted in a particular way. The interpretation is the essence. To say that it is arose as a result of the addition of the New Testament puts the matter backwards: the New Testament could be written only because the scriptures already bore their "Easter" interpretation. Before the church had a New Testament, it already possessed its Old Testament, even though not yet so called. In this second half of our study, therefore, we shall turn over the coin and explore the nature and identity of the Old Testament, as well as problems connected with reading it.

Our subject of inquiry, more precisely, is the new reading or interpretation of Israel's scriptures first discovered, presumably, by Peter and taken over by the Twelve and other followers of the Nazarene, and then by Paul and the other authors of the New Testament. In this reading, they found the images and vocabulary for speaking of Jesus. Thus as Israel's king, Jesus had to be born in Bethlehem (Matthew 2:1, 5-6), where David was born (Micah 5:2). His parents had to flee with the child to Egypt and then be recalled (Matthew 2:13-15), for it was written (Hosea 11:1), "Out of Egypt have I called my son." And drawing on Israel's story of origins (Genesis 3:19), Paul could write that "as by a man came death, by a man has come also the resurrection of the dead. For as in Adam all die, so also in Christ shall all be made alive" (1 Corinthians 15:21-22). This reading of Israel's scriptures is our present concern.

I am calling the second part of this study "The Scriptures of the Gospel" — *of* the gospel, not *for* it. To speak of the scriptures for the gospel might suggest a misrepresentation of what happened, as if that gospel had simply been read off, neutrally and objectively, from the texts of Israel's scriptures, as if the true raison d'être of the scriptures had always been to point to the gospel. To listen to Justin Martyr arguing with his Jewish colleagues,[1] or to many a later Christian, is to listen to just this mistake, as though a Jew must be either blind, stupid, or perverted not to see what is so obvious to a Christian. Such Christians fail to recognize that Jews have continued to read these texts with the closest attention over the centuries without seeing them as pointing to the gospel. They fail as well to acknowledge their own foundations in the highly creative interpretation of Israel's scriptures produced by Peter and his colleagues. The first Bible of the church was not simply the Bible of Israel; it was that Bible read with a new interpretation focused on Christ.

1. See his *Dialogue with Trypho the Jew* from chapter 8 on, with perhaps the climax in chapter 123. We may leave it an open question whether an actual conversation lies behind this mid-second-century composition.

The origin and the nature of the intimate connection between Jesus and Israel's scriptures is portrayed figuratively in Luke's story of the disciples traveling to the village of Emmaus (24:13-35). In that story, the risen Christ, unrecognized, appears to and speaks with two of the disciples, whom he chides for being so slow to understand "all that the prophets have spoken." "Then," Luke's story continues (v. 28), "beginning with Moses and all the prophets, he interpreted to them in all the scriptures the things concerning himself," echoing the Jewish understanding, based on Numbers 12:6-8, that Moses is incomparably the greatest of the prophets. The so-called "christological exegesis of the Old Testament" begins with the Torah, the books of Moses, and so first of all with Genesis. We have seen the importance of the story of the binding of Isaac, and then of the Joseph story, for this interpretation. Then come "all the prophets," of whom David, the presumed author of the Psalms, would prove to be of prime importance.

The Emmaus story, in characteristically scriptural narrative form, tells us, in effect, how the church got its Old Testament and what that Old Testament is. Israel's scriptures, transformed through a new reading, certainly stimulated by the crisis of the preceding weekend, became the scriptures of the Christian church. In order to underscore the transformation, I would call them the Old Testament at this point, even though there was as yet no New Testament bound together with them. The story dramatizes the fact that the Jesus who would come as the risen Christ to the Gentile world would come inseparably from the Jewish scriptures, and the Jewish scriptures would come as the indispensable clothing of Jesus Christ.

The story implies, however, that here are limits to the christological interpretation of the scriptures. "In all the scriptures," so the story goes — that is, selectively — the risen Christ interpreted "the things concerning himself," which is not the same as saying that he interpreted every word of the scriptures as being about himself. "According to the scriptures" does not mean that everything in the scriptures speaks of Christ. As a number of passages in 1 Corinthians show, Paul interpreted more of the scriptures ecclesiologically, as concerning the church primarily, than he did christologically.[2] "These things [the suffering of the Israelites in the wilderness] are warnings for us" (10:6, 11; cf. 10:18). What is written in the Torah is "entirely for our sake" (9:10). "Learn . . . to live according to scripture" (4:6, my translation).

The Emmaus story tells us that the scriptures were interpreted by Jesus Christ, but clearly the agency of Christ was indirect or hermeneutical. The direct agents of the interpretation were the disciples; the hermeneutical key that shaped their work of interpretation was the crucified one. We could say that the disciples were the active agents, Jesus Christ the passive subject, of the interpretation of the scriptures that produced the gospel of Jesus Christ, the Son of God.

As Luke tells his story, the eyes of the disciples "were opened and they recognized" Jesus only when he "took the bread, said the blessing, broke it, and gave it to them," clearly a cultic formulation of the Eucharist. When Jesus then "vanished out of their sight," the disciples recall how moved they were during their conversation on the road, "while he opened for us the scriptures." To have one's eyes opened to see the risen Lord, as this story presents it, is the almost immediate consequence of, hardly distinguishable from, perhaps only another way of speaking of having one's eyes opened to see in all the scriptures the things concerning Jesus Christ. Discovering Jesus as a hermeneutical key to the scriptures is not just discovering something about those scriptures; it is discovering something about Jesus, for it is the discovery of the gospel.

This intimate connection between Jesus and the scriptures, however, is not without its problems, and these show up already in the New Testament. So fully and convincingly did the risen Lord open the scriptures for the church from its very beginning, so well

2. Richard B. Hays, *Echoes of Scripture in the Letters of Paul* (New Haven and London: Yale University Press, 1989), esp. chap. 3, pp. 84-121.

did the church learn in all the scriptures the things concerning Christ, that within perhaps only a generation the church seemed to forget that these were after all, and first of all, the scriptures of continuing and living Israel. It may be that the church of the first century could not conceivably have thought of a continuing Israel, believing as it did that the end of this era was about to arrive, and with it the revelation of Israel's true identity in the followers of Jesus. In any case and increasingly, the church read these texts as if there were no other possible reading of them than its own. It read them in the conviction of being itself Israel, and consequently read the rest of the Jewish people out of the picture, as though quite incidentally, but nonetheless effectively, the Jews had been superseded by the church.

By the end of the Jewish war with Rome, the church had become conscious of what it was doing: an identifiable anti-Jewish note begins to be heard in Mark's Gospel. Was this a reaction to the rejection of the church's interpretation of Israel's scriptures by the overwhelming majority of the Jewish people? Was supersessionism the defensive move of an embattled minority in an inner-Jewish quarrel? For by the time of the destruction of the Temple, it was becoming clear that the church was losing the argument among Jews about the right way to be a Jew. Where the church was not losing was with the Gentiles.

In this complicated situation, at or shortly after the turn of the century, arose perhaps the most enduringly influential theologian of the whole history of the church, Marcion. He appears to have been the only prominent figure in the church of his day to have understood that the scriptures were originally Israel's, that the church's Bible was a Jewish book.[3] From this perfectly sound historical judgment, however, he went on to argue that the church should have nothing to do with this book and that the god of those

---

3. Jaroslov Pelikan, *The Emergence of the Catholic Tradition (100-600),* The Christian Tradition, vol. 1 (Chicago: University of Chicago Press, 1971), 77-78.

scriptures was merely the creator of heaven and earth, a god of justice (and the Law), but not the supreme God and Father of Jesus Christ.[4] Christ had come to reveal this other, previously unknown god (see Acts 17:23), unknown even to the creator god who was the ruler of this age (cf. 1 Corinthians 2:7-8). In Christ had come "the revelation of the mystery which was kept secret for long ages but is now disclosed" (Romans 16:25-26). Convinced that Paul had been the only apostle to have understood Christ, Marcion promoted a collection of some version of ten letters attributed to Paul, together with a short version of Luke's Gospel, as the only proper scriptural collection to be read in the churches.

Marcion succeeded indirectly in restoring Paul to a church perhaps far more given at the time to various Johannine perspectives, and he undoubtedly stimulated the development of the canon of the New Testament. For a time during the early second century, the alternative churches that he founded or led may well have outnumbered the self-styled orthodox churches. In time, however, orthodox opposition to his teaching prevailed, and as a result, the church retained its Old Testament — almost. That is, it retained the full text of the Septuagint as its Bible, but this was supplemented by the books of the New Testament. That might have been nothing but gain for the church, had the scriptures been seen as its source and primer for speaking of Christ, with the New Testament as the early church's copy-book, demonstrating its first attempts to speak of Christ according to those scriptures. That, however, was evidently

---

4. It has usually been thought that Marcion rejected the scriptures just because they were Jewish. This view has been challenged by R. Joseph Hoffmann, *Marcion: On the Restitution of Christianity* (Chico, Calif.: Scholars Press, 1984), who argues that Marcion's real objection to the Old Testament was that it was the revelation of a lesser creator god who did not know the supreme god of love first revealed in Jesus Christ. Marcion took with literal precision Luke 10:22 — "no one" — not even the creator — "knows who the Son is except the Father, or who the Father is except the Son." Any who would argue for the absolute novelty of Jesus Christ may count Marcion as their theological model.

not the legacy that was passed on to the church of succeeding generations.

What the church made of its Old Testament is clearly revealed in its liturgy. As the classic formula says, *lex orandi lex credendi,* or, roughly, "Listen to how we pray and you will discover what we really believe." From its beginning the church has celebrated its gospel with a cultic meal, the Eucharist, so called because its central prayer was a thanksgiving for all God had done for the worshipers, from creation on to its climax in Jesus Christ. This prayer shows that the church sees its whole biblical heritage as a single story, with the life of the worshiping congregation as the latest chapter. It is evidently the most influential location, already established by the second century, of the church's so-called standard canonical narrative,[5] its interpretive guide for reading the Old and New Testaments as a coherent whole.

The fullest versions of the eucharistic prayer are those in Eastern Orthodox liturgies that follow earlier forms reflected in the *Didache* and Hippolytus from the second century. Examples are in the Liturgy of St. James and that of St. Mark.[6] Thanks are offered for creation, especially for the creation of human beings in the image of God, followed by an acknowledgment of human rebellion, leading on to thanksgiving that God did not abandon humanity but sent his Son to the rescue, a rescue to be fully revealed in the future coming of Christ in glory. A more condensed version, however, presumably assuming but making no mention of creation and "the fall," was usual in the West and can be found in the Ordinary of the Mass of the Roman Catholic Church, as well as in the Eliza-

---

5. R. Kendall Soulen defines a canonical narrative as "an interpretive instrument that provides a framework for reading the Christian Bible as a theological and narrative unity" (*The God of Israel and Christian Theology* [Minneapolis: Fortress, 1996], 13). He makes no reference to the eucharistic prayer as its location.

6. All of the liturgical materials can be found in *The Ante-Nicene Fathers: Translations of the Writings of the Fathers down to A.D. 325,* ed. Alexander Roberts and James Donaldson, vol. 7 (reprint, Grand Rapids: Eerdmans, 1970).

77

bethan version of the Prayer Book of the Church of England. Among Eastern Orthodox liturgies, that of St. Adaeus and St. Maris, like the Roman Mass, leaves out anything recognizable from Genesis or from the rest of Israel's story.[7]

The *lex credendi* that appears to follow from all this is that although some parts of the church take seriously the first three chapters of Genesis, they then join the whole church in making a trapeze swing, so to speak, to the opening chapters of the Gospels of Matthew or John. The rest of the Old Testament, from the calling of Abraham and the promise of the land in Genesis 12, through the Exodus and the gift of Torah, through David and the monarchy, Solomon and the Temple, and Elijah and succeeding prophets, to Israel's Wisdom tradition, is in most cases ignored or in a few rites only touched upon. Generally, it appears that the church does not think it need give thanks for the long history of God's dealing with Israel, or of Israel's life with God prior to the coming of Christ. It seems to be content with creation and "the fall," apparently not thinking that the story of what God then did about the situation by calling Abraham and his heirs, and in calling Moses and giving the Torah, is a matter that should concern the church.

What should we make of this evidence? It clearly shows that Marcion's ditheism was overcome: the God and Father of Jesus Christ, according to the post-Marcion church, is also the Creator God of Genesis 1 and 2. The evidence, however, also reveals Marcion firmly in control of the heart of the church's worship, his thesis accepted that the coming of Jesus Christ was a radical novelty. The church seems to agree with Marcion that there is nothing in Israel's story that has anything to teach the church concerning the will and

7. The 1979 Book of Common Prayer also follows the Roman Rite in half of the six alternative forms of the eucharistic prayer that it offers. In its Forms B, C, and D of Rite II, however, mention is made at least of elements of Israel's story, but it is noteworthy that they are touched on as part of the church's story, Israel itself being mentioned only in Form B.

ways of the god it worships. No effort has been made to correct this in even the most recent experiments in liturgical reform.

It is understandable and appropriate for Christians to give God praise and thanks for creation, and to admit that the human family has hardly risen to the occasion, but it is singular that the church takes no notice of the long biblical story of what God then proceeded to do about it. The divine Mother, judging by the most up-to-date Christian liturgies, did no more than the divine Father.[8] If She made a covenant with the descendants of Sarah, and gave to those descendants, through Zipporah's husband, Her holy *Torah,* as a way to live daily life in the land that She had promised to them, so that they might be Her living and caring light to the surrounding nations of the world, if She hovered over Israel with protective maternal care in all the vicissitudes of real life in this real world, it is apparently nothing for which Her church need think it should give praise and thanks. It is no wonder that Episcopalians (on whose proposals for liturgical reform I have drawn) know so little of what they still call the Word of God, when in the central prayer of their worship they are encouraged to count over three-fourths of it as irrelevant for understanding the ways and will of their god.

Any Jew who overhears the church's eucharistic prayer must wonder how far the church is to be trusted when it renounces its old theology of supersessionism. What can Christians be saying when they acknowledge, in statements formally endorsed by their highest governing bodies, that God's covenant with Israel and God's promises to the Jewish people are eternally valid, and then proceed, Eucharist after Eucharist, to ignore both that covenant and those promises? Thoughtful Jews might be excused a measure of skepticism.

---

8. I have in mind, but only as an illustrative example, the *Supplemental Liturgical Materials* prepared by the Standing Liturgical Commission of the Episcopal Church (New York: The Church Pension Fund, 1991; expanded edition, 1996). Its authors' concern for inclusion evidently stops short of Israel, the people of God, the Jewish people.

One cannot assess the status of the Old Testament in the church solely by the Eucharist, of course. In spite of its liturgy, the Old Testament has been available to the church throughout its history and increasingly in the hands and homes of the faithful since the Reformation and Vatican II. Moreover, due to at least some programs of Christian education, some Christians have learned some of the stories that abound from Genesis through 2 Kings. The church would be acting more coherently, however, were it to find an appropriate manner in its liturgy for expressing the foundational character of the Old Testament. This first and largest part of its sacred scripture from which the church derived its gospel, one might think, would be the primary reading when the church gathers around that gospel to worship the God of Israel. In fact, however, the current three-year lectionary followed by major branches of the church hardly reflects this. Indeed, in precisely the season of Easter, when the church celebrates the very beginnings of the gospel that Christ "was raised on the third day in accordance with the scriptures," readings from the Acts of the Apostles are listed as the preferred alternatives to those from the Old Testament.

In the current common lectionary, as in prior lists, the readings from the Old Testament are fairly clearly matched by theme, subject, or wording to the readings from the Gospels or even from the Epistles for the day. This pattern is faithful to and reflects the reading that produced the original gospel. However, the present lectionary selections from the Old Testament are too scanty and scattered to make clear how central and original that reading was. The congregation is not confronted with enough of the text to see that the earliest church's reading was an unusual one; they do not hear the whole text from which certain passages or even words have been taken and given privileged attention. It is as though the church's leadership, without in any way intending to do so, was trying to protect the congregation from seeing its own origins.

Opening the matter to the whole church, however, is precisely what would be healthy for the church of Jesus Christ. The church's gospel originated in and stands or falls with that particular reading of Israel's scriptures which makes them to be the Old Testament. The distinctiveness of that reading is something not to be feared but to be understood and celebrated. How the church lives with its Old Testament is a subject calling for discussion with the fullest possible participation.

Would the introduction of "course reading" of the books of the Old Testament, in which, over successive Sundays, a full book would be read, remedy the problem? It would surely be an improvement. As matters stand, in the course of the full three-year cycle of present readings, only 140 out of over 1200 verses of Exodus are ever heard. As for Genesis, in three years the church hears all of chapter 1, half of chapter 2, one quarter of chapter 3, but the story of the tower of Babel three times. The story of the flood and selections from the story of the covenant with Noah are heard only at the Easter Vigil. In three years, Abraham is heard of four times: eight verses on his call; fifteen verses on God's promises to him; most of the visit of the three angels and Abraham's intercession for the inhabitants of Sodom; and three-quarters of the story of the binding of Isaac. After that, the church in three years hears less than 6 percent of the stories about Jacob and slightly less of the Joseph story. In all, in the three-year cycle, only about five and a half of the fifty chapters of Genesis, chopped into disconnected fragments, are ever read in the church's gathering to hear and celebrate the gospel "according to the scriptures." Compared to this, some "course reading" would be a considerable improvement.

The suggestion has nothing whatsoever to do with trying to make the church "more Jewish," as if that were either desirable or possible. On the contrary, the purpose of this critique and suggestion is entirely Christian, evangelical in the strict sense of the word, and ecclesiological: namely, to make it more possible, more invitational, for the church today to share in and live through again and again that discovery that produced at once the gospel, the Old Testament, and the church. The church can only benefit from rehearsing regularly the particular reading of Israel's scriptures that brought it to birth in the first place. It might even lead to uncovering new or neglected aspects of the gospel for our own time. Indeed, the gospel might again appear new, if it were discovered anew, as it was in the church's beginning, to be the gospel "according to the scriptures."

A cursory survey of the present status of the Old Testament in the church suggests that its standing is weak. With a gospel derived from scriptures that are themselves either ignored or put in second place, one might suspect that the gospel itself would be weakened, being in danger of being replaced by some other message according more with the current experience of today's church. The past two centuries in the life of the church indicates that the danger is real and serious enough to call for some basic rethinking about the Old Testament.

CHAPTER 8

The Old Testament, not Tanak or Hebrew Bible

A REEVALUATION OF THE OLD TESTAMENT and its role in the church should begin by recognizing that it is not the same entity as the Tanak, the Bible of the Jewish people. It is also not the Hebrew Bible of the community of biblical scholars. Superficially, these are all one text, if we ignore the differences of language and the more striking difference of the order of the books within them. In actual use, however, that one text is in fact three, each belonging to one of three different communities, each read and valued for distinctively different purposes and subjected to different canons of interpretation. In this chapter, I want to make this clear, so that it can be seen in what sense and with what implications the sacred scriptures of the Christian church from its very beginnings were and were not the scriptures of ancient Israel that remain the sacred scriptures of the Jewish people.

Before turning to the two communities for which these writings are sacred scriptures, I shall begin with the scholarly or academic community and its text, the Hebrew Bible.[1] For the academic com-

---

1. On this, see Brevard S. Childs, *Introduction to the Old Testament as Scripture* (Philadelphia: Fortress, 1979), 659-71.

munity today, the Hebrew Bible is the primary text of ancient Israel's life, history, and religion. In this setting, the text is therefore primarily a historical document, although it can also be regarded as a literary production to be read as a classic. Those members of the academic community who have an interest in this text may or may not have any sympathy for either or both of the contemporary Jewish and Christian communities, but they have set themselves the task of understanding their document from the perspective of its authors, or their sources, or later editors, or even of those who collected and arranged the various parts together in what came to be the canons of later communities.[2] Theirs is essentially a historical discipline, and they read and interpret this collection of writings as historical documents. They are concerned with them in the past tense: why they were written, what they meant, how they came to be in the canon. The scholarly study of the Bible is a fascinating one, especially today in light of new historical evidence and new methods. For these scholars, however, the investigation of how the Bible has been understood and used by those for whom it is sacred scripture would be a study of postbiblical times. Such an investigation falls outside of their area of research.

The Jewish community of today, on the other hand, has before it something else: the story of its origins and the storehouse of its ancient and ever-living memories and hopes. It has before it above all the Torah of Sinai, its original and enduring charter and constitution as a people and as a nation, read in synagogues every Shabbat throughout the year as its guide for walking, halakah, and its bond with God. The Jewish community reads Deuteronomy 5:3 as if it were written today: "It was not with our fathers that the LORD made

2. These and the following generalizations about the academic study of the Hebrew Bible have in view primarily the academic scene in the United States and also in Israel. They would have to be modified for the German scene, where it is still the case that Christian clergy receive their theological education in state universities, from theological professors who are regular members of the faculty and paid from state funds.

this covenant, but with us, the living, every one of us who is here today" (JPS).

As is the case with any constitution of a living community, the Torah of Moses has needed continual interpretation to take account of new situations, and the Jewish people have therefore lived by the so-called Oral Torah, the Mishnah and Talmud, as well as by centuries of Responsa literature (collections of authoritative decisions by rabbinic courts or eminent rabbis). The different so-called denominations of Judaism today represent variant views of that classical tradition of interpretation, but the Jewish community as a whole sees its Bible as a collection of books that remains alive through fresh interpretation in the light of and as a response to ever new events of Jewish history.

The Jewish tradition values right behavior over right belief, and since study is also prized, Jews have generally turned to the Bible for instruction, the basic question being not what is to be known, and certainly not what is to be believed, but what is to be done and how. This accounts in part for the central place given to the Five Books of Moses in the Jewish liturgy, since they contain Israel's first codes for living. Jews turn to the Bible, however, not just generally for instruction but as God's Torah quite specifically for the Jewish people. Torah may have been God's original intention for how all people ought to live, according to one rabbinic interpretation, but all the other nations of the world refused to accept it; only Israel agreed to live by it.[3] Quite early in the development of Judaism, in the time of the Hadrianic persecutions following the Bar Kokhba revolt (132-35 c.e.), the students of Rabbi Akiva developed the teaching that God also had provided a Torah for the nations, the Gentiles: the seven Noachide commandments. These rabbis and their successors taught that if a Gentile were to live a life

3. For an old version of this tradition, see Jacob Z. Lauterbach, ed. and trans., *Mekilta de-Rabbi Ishmael: A Critical Edition,* 3 vols. (Philadelphia: Jewish Publication Society, 1973), 2:234-47.

in obedience to those few commandments, that person was to count as righteous and would surely have a place in the world to come.[4] Israel, however, was given the full Torah, which no Gentile was obligated to follow, with the result that the Torah is for Jews the specific word of God to them, God's instruction as to how Jews are to live their life with God so as to be God's partners in mending this dangerously threatened world. The Torah might even be seen as God's and Israel's *Ketubbah,* their marriage contract.

Against this background, we can now define and appreciate the particularity of the sacred scriptures of the church, namely, its Old Testament. The church's Old Testament differs from the Bible of the Jewish people in the order of its books, in the list (in some churches) of books it contains, and above all in being used always in translation.[5] It begins, as does the Tanak, with the Pentateuch, the Five Books of Moses, but the prophetic writings (which in the Tanak include Joshua through 2 Kings and come next) appear at the end of the collection. Between come most of the "Writings," which make up the third and final section of the Jewish Bible. Since the Gentile church from the beginning used the Septuagint, large parts of the church to this day have retained several of the books of that translation which were not preserved in the Hebrew Bible of the Jewish people. The Greek church uses the Greek Septuagint itself, but elsewhere the text has been translated into the local language.

The church did not inherit its Old Testament. As I have argued, the Old Testament arose as the particular interpretation of Israel's scriptures that brought the church into existence, so it is misleading

4. A thorough study of the origin and development of the so-called Noachide Covenant has been produced by Klaus Müller, *Tora für die Völker: Die noachidischen Gebote und Ansätze zu ihrer Rezeption im Christentum* (Berlin: Institut Kirche und Judentum, 1994).

5. In Christian congregations in Israel, of course, Hebrew, the local national language, is used by Hebrew-speaking Israeli Christians. Consequently, they read the Old Testament and also the New Testament in Hebrew.

to say either that the church wrote (and so precedes) the Bible, or that the Bible precedes the church. In discovering the gospel "according to the scriptures," Peter and his colleagues, by that very process, discovered the scriptures that would be the church's own, the reading of Israel's scriptures that made them ineradicably the church's Old Testament.

As I have argued, the disciples' interpretation of their scriptures was forged in their need to understand the shattering event of the crucifixion of Jesus as *rex iudaeorum*. As the Jewish Bible is Israel's scriptures interpreted out of the further experience of the Jewish people (wars with Rome, the destruction of the Temple and of Jerusalem, and the reconstruction of Jewish life by the rabbis of the first and second centuries), so the church's Old Testament is those same scriptures interpreted out of the church's particular experience. Both communities shaped their sacred scriptures from the same tradition but according to two different histories. The results were as different as were those histories.

The difference between the Jewish and the Christian reading of the scriptures is not rightly expressed by saying that Christians read it figuratively or typologically, whereas Jews read it historically. The so-called christological and ecclesiological interpretation of many passages that characterizes the church's reading of the Old Testament is at once the ground and the consequence of the conviction that in these texts Christians find themselves addressed in the present moment by the Word of God. But that, as I pointed out, is just how Jews have always read such passages as Deuteronomy 5:3.

It is important to recognize that both Christians and Jews read this text with an interpretation, so long as we realize that there is no alternative. Whenever someone presumes to define "what the Bible really says," it is always appropriate to point out that the Bible has no lips or tongue, that what the Bible says can be heard only from the interpreting mouth of some Jew or some Christian, or some biblical scholar, for that matter. The Jewish tradition hears this text as God's word of liberating and loving instruction or command. The Christian cannot hear it in quite the same way, since God's word of liberation and love, as the Christian hears it, comes inseparably from the figure of Jesus. The Jewish people hear it as they do because it speaks of and from their founding moment at Sinai. But Sinai was not the founding moment of the Christian church. For Christians, their invitation into the story of the Bible comes in the form of the gospel concerning the Jew of Nazareth, so inevitably they hear the story always as leading up to him. He invites them to the reading of Israel's story as his own story. In telling of Israel, Israel's story for Christians always tells of Christ. Those are two irreducibly different readings, two different interpretations of the biblical text.

Since neither Christians nor Jews are able to read this text as the other does, each community has either ignored the other or concluded that the other is simply wrong. No alternative was entertained seriously by either side from the partings of the ways in the second half of the first until the second half of the twentieth century. With the reversal in official church teaching concerning the Jewish people, however, a reversal marked by major teaching documents of both the Catholic and Protestant churches,[6] the question can and must be reopened on both sides. I leave it to Jews to address the question as they see fit. On the Christian side, the question is: what is possible for Christians to say about the Old Testament, now that the churches have also acknowledged the Jewish people as the continuing people of God's original and unbroken covenant?

6. For a summary of such documents, see Paul van Buren *A Theology of the Jewish-Christian Reality. Part 1: Discerning the Way* (New York: Seabury, 1981; reprint, Lanham, Md.: University Press of America, 1995), 174-75. For further detail, see Allan Brockway, Rolf Rendtorff, Simon Schoon, and Paul van Buren, *The Teaching of the Churches and the Jewish People* (Geneva: World Council of Churches, 1988). See also Clark M. Williamson, *A Guest in the House of Israel: Post-Holocaust Church Theology* (Louisville, Ky.: Westminster/John Knox, 1993), 30ff., to whom I owe the term "teaching documents" as a designation for these statements.

To start with, Christians can and must reaffirm what they have said from the beginning: the scriptures of Israel read as the Old Testament tell the story that they understand themselves to have been invited to call their own. To be a Christian has always meant to regard Abraham as one's father — today we would add: and to regard Sarah as one's mother. The church has never had a Bible that did not begin with the book of Genesis. Christians have been traditionally brought up on the stories of Joseph and his brothers, the Exodus, the Ten Commandments from Sinai, and King David, and their primary hymn book has always been the Psalter. The church has at least claimed that this is its own book; it is difficult to see how it could be itself without continuing to do so.

It is, however, not simply the church's own book. Rather — and this should have been seen and said from the beginning — it is *also* the church's book. This book is about the church, but not in the way that it is about the Jewish people; it is about the church by way of anticipation. Abraham is on the way to being the father of many nations, and Sarah is on the way to being their mother. The ground for this claim is the gospel "according to the scriptures," and the conviction that in Christ the promises to Abraham began to be realized also in those called by God to be members of Christ's body. In Christ, so Christians believe, his God becomes their God and his people their people. Consequently, the story of God's people with God, and of God with God's people, is always the church's story too.

That "too" is decisive, despite the church's failure to see it for nineteen centuries. It is decisive because, on its own grounds of trust in its incorporation into Christ, and in its own self-interest in holding to its unity with him who gave himself "for us," the church must insist that the biblical story, because it is his, is first of all Israel's, and that the covenant of which it speaks is first of all Israel's — and by "Israel" the church should be clear that it means most explicitly to include the Jewish people of today. If the Jewish people of today are not the continuing Israel of which the Old Testament speaks, then neither is the Christian church of today in any of its branches the continuing apostolic church of which the New Testament speaks, and for exactly the same reasons. If there is a continuity in the one case, through all the historical changes, then there is also continuity in the other, grounded in both cases in its calling, its election, its memory, and its hope. Any argument that would deny that continuity in the case of the people Israel would also nullify it for the church of Jesus Christ.

Further, the church must, in its own self-interest and on its own grounds, insist that the first, the original, and therefore also the continuing addressee of its scriptures was and is the Jewish people. The covenant endures; God's election stands. If the church denies that, it deprives itself of the most concrete and enduring sign and sacrament of God's reliable involvement in this world. If God is not faithful to God's original people, if God does not keep promises, then what grounds would the church have to hope that God will be faithful to it? In its own self-interest, the church should be expected to maintain that the scriptures are Israel's first of all, and only then also the church's, and that they can only address Gentile Christians because they address Israel, the Jewish people, first of all.

The church's acknowledgment that its Old Testament is first of all the Bible of the Jews detracts in no way from its being also the word of God for the church. Christians as well as Jews can be addressed by these writings. By stressing the "also," Christians can acknowledge the Jewishness of these writings and the authenticity of Jewish readings of them, without in any way abandoning that reading of them which is distinctively its own.

From its beginning and throughout its history, the church has heard God's words of comfort and promise, and also God's words of reprimand, addressed to Israel in the scripture, as being also words spoken to the nations gathered in — and also outside — the church. Whenever it thinks it hears them as words addressed only to the church, it is taking Marcion's false path. When it dares to believe itself included in God's words to Israel, however, it hears an authentic biblical message: God's word to Israel was from the beginning to Israel-singled-out-from-among, and chosen-on-behalf-of, the nations.[7]

Christians can say that in the scriptures they hear the word of the God of Israel, but they hear that God as one on the way to do a new thing. Jews might agree that God's covenant is always in need of renewal because God's people, like God's church, is always in need of renewal. Christians believe, however, as no Jew on Jewish grounds need, that Jesus, and the Gentile church that heard in him the call of the God of Israel, was just such a new thing. In making this claim, however, the church should also grant that the word of God which it sees embodied in Jesus is also the word of the God who is still on the way to do new things. The story beginning with Abraham is not over. It is not over for the Jewish people, not over for the church, not over for the world, and, especially, not over for God. That is not at all the same as to say that the story is all over except for its culmination in "the day of the LORD." Rather, the story continues because it is, so obviously, nowhere near its end.

There is a final implication to the Christian confession that the Old Testament is also and first of all the Jewish Bible: when Christians confess that this book is the living word of the living God, they imply that it is the word of a god who also has a history. The church has joined the Jewish people in the latter's confession that God is one, but Christians as well as Jews have tended to conceive of God's unity as beyond time and space. Both Jews and Christians might do some fresh thinking here. If our best conception of God is personal, then God's unity may be conceived as personal. A personal god, to hear the witness of the scriptures, is one who

---

7. On the importance of Israel's calling for the sake of the nations in Israel's scriptures, especially in the Torah, see Friedrich-Wilhelm Marquardt, *Das christliche Bekenntnis zu Jesus, dem Juden,* 2 vols. (Munich: Kaiser, 1990-91), vol. 1, §3, esp. 178-89; also Marquardt, *Von Elend und Heimsuchung zur Dogmatik: Prolegomena zur Dogmatik* (Munich: Kaiser, 1988), 454ff.

can love, be angry, forgive, and promise. But a personal god will also be a god who can love my parents before I was born, love me today without betraying my parents, and love my children after me without betraying me. God can make an everlasting covenant with Israel, generation after generation: those "begats" of Genesis 4, 5, and 10 introduce the story of God's eternal covenant with Abraham and his descendants. Further, such a god can also call Gentiles into his service at a later time. And God alone knows what may be yet in store for the future. One God means one story, one history of God with God's creation, a history always open to novelty, just as it is always open to risk and danger, for God as well as for creation. God too has a history.

If Jews and Christians believe that God is one, then it is up to them to see each new thing that they believe God has done as a part of God's continuing history and so as confirming and renewing, not denying or shutting off, what God has done before. Is that not what both Jews and Christians mean by the faithfulness of God? And that is surely what Paul claimed in his powerful, concise summary of his great, last letter (Romans 15:8-9, my translation): "For I tell you that Christ became a servant of the Jewish people for the sake of God's truthfulness, in order to confirm the promises to the patriarchs, so that the Gentiles might glorify God for his mercy."

A few years ago, I wrote an essay with the title "On Reading Someone Else's Mail: The Church and Israel's Scriptures,"[8] arguing that the church has a right to read the Old Testament only in acknowledging that its message is also and first of all addressed to the Jewish people. The thesis needs to be qualified by the recognition that in fact the church never read the scriptures with a sense that it was reading someone else's mail, and that is because Peter and his

8. Paul van Buren, "On Reading Someone Else's Mail: The Church and Israel's Scriptures," in *Die Hebräische Bibel und ihre zweifache Nachgeschichte: Festschrift für Rolf Rendtorff zum 65. Geburtstag*, ed. Erhard Blum, Christian Macholz, and Ekkehard W. Stegemann, 595-606 (Neukirchen-Vluyn: Neukirchener Verlag, 1990).

fellow discoverers of the gospel read them as their own Jewish mail, albeit with eyes made new by their desperate need, on that "first day of the week," to understand the crucifixion of Jesus of Nazareth as King of the Jews. And those to whom they taught their gospel learned that new reading along with that gospel: the scriptures so read were always for them "addressed to us," that is, to themselves. Only as the church became increasingly Gentile did "the Jews" come into focus as others not sharing the church's reading. After centuries of denying the validity of Judaism and of Jewish readings of the scriptures, the church now seeks to affirm the Jewish people and their covenant, and so also to affirm Jewish readings of the scriptures. It is therefore too simple to say that in reading its Old Testament the church is reading someone else's mail. What can be said is that in reading its Old Testament, the church has become aware that it is reading what is also being read as Tanak by Jews.

This awareness leaves us with a major problem. After insisting for centuries that the Jewish and Christian readings of the scriptures of ancient Israel were incompatible, how can we now argue that both are right? If the church affirms the Jewish reading, can it continue what has been called a christological interpretation of the Old Testament, which is nothing other than the church's reading of its scriptures? At this point the dreaded specter of a typological reading of the scriptures looms on the horizon, and we must now face up to this monster, to see whether it is as dreadful as it is so often portrayed.

CHAPTER 9

On the Art of Reading the Old Testament

THE OLD TESTAMENT IS the scripture of Israel read as the framework, context, and anticipation of the story of Jesus Christ. Not every word points to Christ, but, as the Emmaus story illustrates, the scriptures as a whole, in this reading, pertain to him. The early church's central affirmations concerning Jesus were derived from and formulated in accordance with those scriptures. I have been calling this a christological reading of the scriptures of ancient Israel. The Old Testament consists in just this reading, and a christological reading is what makes the Old Testament to be the first, longest, and foundational part of the church's Bible.

In Chapter 3 we looked at examples of the remarkably similar messianic reading of some postbiblical Jews from before the time of the beginning of the church. The words of the prophet Nathan in 2 Samuel 7:11-14 were, as we saw, read by some Jews as referring not to Solomon, David's actual son, but to an unidentified future descendant whose rule God would establish and bless. The passage was read, that is, as a promise not yet fulfilled, as referring to events soon to occur. The difference between a messianic reading and a christological one is that the former looks to one who is still to come, whereas the latter identifies the promised one of the text with Jesus of Nazareth. Other examples, such as Psalm 2:7 ("You are my son, today I have begotten you") and Psalm 110:1 ("The LORD says to my lord, 'Sit at my right hand, till I make your enemies your footstool'"), reveal the same difference. A christological reading depends upon, but is an adaptation of, existing messianic readings, applied specifically to Jesus of Nazareth.

Once the gospel according to the scriptures had been discovered and messianic readings were turned into christological ones, new christological readings were discovered, an example of which is Matthew's reading (1:23) or misreading of Isaiah 7:14 ("Behold, a young woman shall conceive and bear a son," which for its author served perhaps only to mark a short span of time before the coming of the threatening "day" of divine retribution). The so-called Servant Songs of Second Isaiah provided the post-New Testament church with a series of texts that were read christologically.[1]

A christological reading of specific texts, as we have pointed out, is based on reading Israel's story as the key to understanding Jesus, or of telling his story as the story of Israel. Although for many centuries Israel's story was read by Christians as though it had no other meaning than this, such a narrowing is not necessary to a christological reading. Israel's story can also be read as Israel's story in its own right, and then, in addition, as being the key to the story of Jesus, and of course a christological reading opens the way to an ecclesiological one as well, as Paul's letters demonstrate. The text, on such a reading, can speak directly to the present situation of the reader and the reader's community. Such is evidently the normal way in which texts held to be sacred are read in communities that so regard them.

Messianic, christological, and ecclesiological readings of Israel's

---

1. Many of these have been made familiar to even biblically illiterate Christians through Handel's *Messiah*.

scriptures are all cases of seeing one entity (e.g., the future messiah, Christ, or the church) in another (e.g., David's son, or Israel), of letting one entity stand for another. In this broad sense, they are all special cases of a typological reading. The present antitype is interpreted in the light of the scriptural type. As Isaac carried the wood for his own sacrifice, so, according to two midrashim,[2] every Jew crucified by the Romans carried his own cross, and Christians applied the type to Jesus. As Israel was rescued through water (the Sea of Reeds and the cloud — so Paul[3]), so Christians are rescued through the water of baptism, baptism being the antitype, the Exodus from Egypt being the type. Typological reading is a means of showing that whatever was written in the sacred text "was written for our sake" (1 Corinthians 7:10).

Many today, including many Christians and Jews, hesitate to follow, much less adopt, any form of typological reading, even though this was the method of interpretation of the sacred texts that nourished the Jewish and Christian traditions from their beginnings. The reason for this hesitation is less clear than its existence. A common reason given is that a typological interpretation treats the text in an unhistorical manner, the assumption being that ancient texts should be read in their historical context, their meaning being the one that the author had in mind, or one that his or her original audience would have seen in the text. To whomever the author of the Servant Songs of Second Isaiah may have been referring, for example, it was certainly not, we feel quite sure, to some messianic figure of the postbiblical period, least of all to Jesus of Nazareth. To refer this or any similar texts to later figures or events is unhistorical, and that, so the argument goes, is why one should not engage in typological exegesis.

2. *Genesis Rabbah* 56:3 and *Pesiqta Rabbati* 31:2. I have these references from Sebastian Brock, "Two Syriac Verse Homilies on the Binding of Isaac," *Le Muséon: Revue d'Études Orientales* 99 (1986): 95n.

3. 1 Corinthians 10:1-2.

It may be, however, that those ancient methods of exegesis are not so foreign to us as first appears. A historical reading certainly has it place and legitimacy, but it is more suited to the work of biblical scholars than to the communities of either Jews or Christians, for whom the texts are sacred. Within these communities, a historical reading is hardly normative, as their liturgical practice amply illustrates. Liturgies function precisely by reading and offering up ancient prayers on the assumption that they are appropriate in the present, week after week and year after year. This is all the more true of the reading of the portion of Torah in the synagogue each Shabbat, and of the lessons from the Old Testament, the Epistles, and the Gospels read at each Eucharist. In many Christian traditions, such reading is attended and responded to as "the Word of the Lord," a word that is believed to be in some sense a present expression of the divine. A merely historical reading could only express what ancient authors believed about themselves, their people, or their god.

Within the Christian tradition, the Protestant churches especially have developed a conception and practice of the sermon that depends on the acknowledged conviction that the biblical text is potentially always renewably relevant.[4] The admittedly ancient text can "come alive," so to speak, and address the church in each new situation. When the text is so read and expounded, its meaning is bound neither to the intention of its author nor to the reception of its first readers. It is, with Paul, a reading that expresses the conviction that "it was written for our sake" (1 Corinthians 9:10), that "these things happened to them as a warning, but they were written down for our instruction" (1 Corinthians 10:11). My conclusion is that Jews and Christians, in their actual practice, are by no means as restricted to a historical reading of sacred tests as our initial worries suggested. Indeed, a privileged status of that reading is itself open to question.

4. On this see Karl Barth, *Church Dogmatics*, 13 vols., eds. G. W. Bromiley and T. F. Torrance (Edinburgh: T & T Clark, 1936-75), I/1, §4, but also I/2, §21.

The exegesis of Jesus' disciples that produced the gospel was, like much Jewish exegesis of the period, driven by events difficult for them to comprehend. For other Jews such imponderables included the deaths of noble martyrs, the desecration of God's Temple, and the triumph of Israel's enemies. The exegesis of the disciples was driven by events fully as incomprehensible for them. Theirs was neither the first nor the last case of turning to the scriptures in the hope of wresting from them some understanding of the incomprehensible.

A modern sense of discomfort with the typological exegetical method of New Testament authors, as of other postbiblical Jews, may in fact be due less to a difference of method and more to the different circumstances driving the respective interpretations. They worked under the pressure of an event in their time that was truly oxymoronic, that of a crucified Messiah. We do our exegesis, at least always in part, under the pressure of the oxymoronic character of our existence in our own time: that of presuming to be Christians, or Jews for that matter, in the midst of an all-pervasive secular culture.

This, I believe, is the heart of a modern resistance to typological exegesis. For good and understandable reasons, the secularist in each of us prefers to see each thing as itself and as standing for itself alone. If illness can be demon possession, if a sound investment can be the result of a divine blessing, we are inhibited from tracking the physiological cause of the illness or from planning investment strategies. Much of the progress in science, medicine, and economic development in recent centuries has depended on *not* seeing things typologically.

The pervasive influence of a secular preference for letting each entity stand only for itself explains the primary difficulty in understanding the gospel that was taught to Paul. The difficulty is not how the gospel was discovered out of and found to be according to the scriptures. The problem lies in the metaphysical or religious convictions that make it possible to speak of one person's death as being "for our sins." That assertion is the epitome of letting one entity stand for another. As we have seen, behind it stands the figure of Isaac's death being counted for the benefit of his descendants. In a secular culture, it is difficult to make room for the idea that blessings can follow for future generations, regardless of whether they be descendants by blood or by faith, from the one righteous deed or faith of a patriarch. We are so much the children of the individualism of our culture that we have trouble finding that compelling. How much more congenial is the word of Jeremiah (31:29-30), "In those days they shall no longer say: 'The fathers have eaten sour grapes, and the children's teeth are set on edge.' But every one shall die for his own sins; each man who eats sour grapes, his teeth shall be set on edge."

Jeremiah certainly has his place in Israel's history and in its sacred literature, but at least in the passage just cited, he was not speaking for the preponderance of Israel's tradition. Underlying the tradition and practice of the Temple sacrificial cult is the idea that one person's death may offset the sins of others. That cult produced no definitive theory of how a death could be a compensation for someone's sin. It was sufficient that God had provided Israel with this cult, so that the people would have something to do in the face of ruptured relations with their God. Behind the sacrificial system stood, more broadly, the strong sense of communal solidarity of which the passage from Jeremiah takes no account. And finally, perhaps at the deepest level, the saying against which Jeremiah wrote is grounded in the stories in Genesis of the blessings of the fathers coming upon their children. To dismiss those stories is to abandon much that defines Israel's tradition and shaped her scriptures.

If Jeremiah does not speak for the biblical tradition, however, he does speak to the individualism of Western culture. One could argue, of course, that common behavior reveals more dependence and interdependence than that individualism implies. In a study two decades ago on the sacrificial death of Christ, the English biblical scholar Frances Young gave many examples from today that illustrate how the deeds of one person can have consequences for the many.[5] I do think, however, that the biblical view of human solidarity remains difficult for people today to make their own.

There is, nevertheless, a consolation and even a reward if Jews and Christians would face this difficulty together. Although their present reading of their scriptures may be driven to a large extent by the pressure of a secular culture, with its debilitating individualism as well as its healthy respect for the particularity of each entity, they can hardly ignore that as Jews and Christians they read differently even the text that they share. This fact could lead them to see that they are, as Jews and Christians, still informed by the interpretations that shaped their two traditions back in the days of their beginning. It appears that their differences as Christians and Jews matter to them, and those differences are rooted in the first century of the Common Era and have little to do with the pressure of our secular culture today. The two distinct interpretive traditions were largely set for both communities by at least the second century. Both communities are still sufficiently under the influence of those interpretive developments as to leave no doubt on either side that they cherish and respect those developments that created the differences between them. We are, evidently, far from being merely the creatures of our time.

The principle alternative to typological interpretations of the scriptures is one that we have called historical. If we read the classic messianic text, 2 Samuel 7:12-14, historically, what do we learn? (1) David is promised that his own biological son ("I will raise up your offspring after you, who shall come forth from your body") (2) will reign in David's stead ("and I shall establish his kingdom"). (3) That son, obviously Solomon, shall build the Temple ("He shall build a house for my name"), and consequently (4) a bit of Hebrew hyperbole is in order ("and I will establish the throne of his kingdom

5. Frances M. Young, *Sacrifice and the Death of Christ* (Philadelphia: Westminster, 1975). See especially Chap. 6.

for ever"). And further, (5) "I will be his father, and he shall be my son": stock monarchical formulae of the ancient Near East. So much for a historical reading of the text. It contains some mundane information, but it is hardly of contemporary interest for either a Jew or a Christian.

Remembering that the Jewish tradition sees the Torah in part as the fundamental law or constitution of Israel as a people, we may ponder the interesting parallel with the Constitution of the United States and recall that a historical reading of that document has never gone unchallenged and has seldom prevailed. What was in the mind of its authors, "the intention of the framers," has not been able to win a controlling role in its exegesis. Lincoln's radical interpretation at Gettysburg, "a nation conceived in liberty and dedicated to the proposition that all men are created equal," brought forth a sneering editorial from the "historicizing" Chicago *Times* of the day, reminding its readers that none of the framers had any idea of the equality of men of different races.[6] Historically, the editorial may have been correct. Lincoln's exegesis prevailed.

If, then, typological reading is less a problem than at first appears, there remains the difficulty that two different communities of interpretation have read the common sacred text in such a way as to point ahead to two different futures. One community has read the passage from 2 Samuel 7 as pointing to a king who has yet to appear; the other has read it as pointing to a most nonroyal "king," Jesus of Nazareth, who has come but whose kingdom remains in the future.

Merely to mention this classic difference between the Jewish and Christian readings of Israel's scriptures raises the crucial question for both communities today, whether it could ever be legitimate in either community to read the scriptures as pointing ahead to two different futures, whether biblical types could be read as having two

6. Gary Wills, *Lincoln at Gettysburg: The Words That Remade America* (New York: Simon & Schuster, 1992), 38-39.

different but perhaps related antitypes. This question did not arise so long as each community claimed for itself alone the rightful inheritance of Abraham and Israel. The question is unavoidable, however, once it is acknowledged, on whichever side, that both communities are legitimate heirs. Since the Christian churches began to affirm the eternal election of the Jewish people and the validity of the continuing Sinai covenant, a dual typology has been at least implicit if not developed.

In his *Dialogue with Trypho,* Justin Martyr presented the problem, without resolving it, by saying to his Jewish colleague, "As therefore from the one man Jacob, who was surnamed Israel, all your nation has been called Jacob and Israel; so we from Christ, who begat us unto God, like Jacob, and Israel, and Judah, and Joseph, and David, are called and are the true sons of God, and keep the commandments of Christ."[7] It seems clear from the context that Justin, although primarily concerned to demonstrate the validity of the Christian calling and so the church's right to the name Israel, thought the claim to this name was one which the Jewish people had surrendered. But we need not follow him at this point. We might say, instead, that whether by genuine physical descent from Jacob/Israel, or by spiritual union with Christ as the confirmation of Israel, both communities have every right to interpret every scriptural address to the Israelites of old as also addressed to them. Both, in short, can see themselves as heirs of Abraham and the promises of God made to him.

Such a dual reading of Israel's scriptures may be justified by following Justin in appealing to its coherence with historical developments. Justin justified the church's claim to the name of Israel by

7. Justin Martyr, *Dialogue with Trypho the Jew* 123. The translation is from Alexander Roberts and James Donaldson, eds., *The Ante-Nicene Fathers: Translations of the Writings of the Fathers down to A.D. 325,* vol. 1 (reprint; Grand Rapids: Eerdmans, 1973), 261. The date of the *Dialogue* would seem to be not long after the second Jewish war with Rome (ended 135 C.E.), to which Justin refers in Chaps. 1 and 9.

its continuing life with God: "from Christ begotten unto God, called true sons of God, keeping the commandments of Christ," just as the Jewish people had a right to the name by descent from Jacob/Israel. If it is acknowledged, however, that there is not just one community that continues to live from the biblical story and is its bearer through time, but two such communities, then a dual reading of that story is the only one that will bear witness to this fact.

The conviction that there are two witnessing communities has been expressed with increasing clarity in the teaching documents produced and promulgated by the highest authorities of an increasing number of churches over the past forty years. A perusal of these documents reveals that something more is happening than mere secular fatigue with religious rivalry and tension. The call for a new understanding of god, of the scriptures, and of Christian traditions is clearly grounded in deep reflection on the grounds of tradition itself. The conviction, moreover, is not one-sided. An equally clear statement has come from the Jewish side, in the stunning thesis enunciated in the 1988 *Statement of Principles of Conservative Judaism:* "Theological humility requires us to recognize that although we have but one God, God has more than one nation."[8]

No Christian could read that statement, surely more than a match for the declaration *Nostra Aetatae* of Vatican II, with anything but profound appreciation for the courage its formulation expresses. Nevertheless, I should like to make more explicit what is implicit in it: namely, that theological humility is and can only be grounded in one's deepest convictions about what God has been up to and is still up to in this world. Theological humility must mean that Jews and Christians stand together before the God of Israel and confess that they have long held a far too limited view of God and God's ways. Theological humility can only mean that one has become

8. *Emet ve Emunah: Statement of Principles of Conservative Judaism* (New York: Jewish Theological Seminary of America, 1988), 43.

aware that one's theology is in need of correction. If it has been certain facts of recent history that have led some of us to see this, that is only how it has always been in each stage of the growth and development of both communities and their exegetical practices. With theological humility, then, we turn to reconsider our theology in the light of a dual reading of Israel's scriptures to which we are forced by the dual history of God's people Israel and God's church. On the Christian side, it is well to recall what is at stake in attempting such a dual exegetical path. At stake is whether the church that was against the people Israel for nineteen centuries is in fact giving way to a church that is for the people Israel.

CHAPTER 10

Who Then Is the Beloved Son, and Whose?

LIKE REBEKAH (Genesis 25:19-26), Second Temple Judaism gave birth to twins: Christianity and Rabbinic Judaism. The LORD's word to Rebekah in that story (v. 23) could be applied also to these later twins: "Two . . . separate peoples shall issue from your body. One people shall be mightier than the other, and the older shall serve the younger" (JPS). Except for the inapplicable last clause, the saying describes what happened to the twin children of Second Temple Judaism. The story of Jesus of Nazareth and the gospel concerning him were told from the beginning "according to the scriptures" by a people who lived from that telling. More or less contemporaneously, formative Rabbinic Judaism took shape also according to those same scriptures. Each historical development was, of course, built on a selective use of those scriptures, and both developments constituted — and were constituted by — a distinctive interpretation of those texts. The interpretations were, however, different, and each in its own way came to be understood as denying the legitimacy of the other.

Both Jews and Christians should realize that the other tradition also sees itself as having arisen "according to the scriptures." Each of these two communities defines its identity as grounded, directly or indirectly, in the story of Abraham's beloved son Isaac, and both read that tale as the story of the self-sacrifice and restoration of Isaac for the benefit of his descendants. For all the changes through which both communities have passed over the centuries, this grounding of identity remains common to them.

Honesty, however, requires a major qualification. Today, a fair number of those who still call themselves Christian, and many more baptized who no longer do, find the idea of an atoning death at best a puzzle, and hardly good news. The thought of Christ as Isaac and of his death as a sacrifice is more strange than outrageous to them. The words "Christ, our paschal lamb, has been sacrificed" (1 Corinthians 5:7) are alien to many who still see Jesus as a model or ideal, though hardly "according to the scriptures." The biblical story of the beloved son is by no means the ground of their identity, even if they think of themselves as Christians in some sense.

Likewise, there is probably an even higher proportion of Jews who want no part of the *aqedah,* however interpreted, except to insist that its only significance is to show that their ancestors long ago rejected every form of human sacrifice. By birth, by heritage, perhaps by some external pressure, they remain Jews, but many secularized and assimilated Jews are repelled by the very notion of chosenness and certainly do not find their identity in the story of the binding of Isaac, much less in that story retold as the self-sacrifice of the beloved son.

Therefore, today we should think not simply of two groups, Jews and Christians, but of at least four broad groups of Jews and Christians, cutting across all denominational and other lines. Two of them, which we have just identified, accept neither the original story of Genesis 22 nor its first-century interpretation as in any way important for them, and they would refuse to see either as even relevant to their identity, much less as defining it. Secular Jews may see it as part of their folklore, hardly to be taken seriously today;

somewhat secularized Christians and most ex-Christians, if they are aware of the story at all, would perhaps regard it as a bit of primitive mythology long since left behind and well forgotten. Neither of these two groups believes that it is the beloved son (or daughter), or, for that matter, that god, if such there be, even has beloved sons or daughters.

Of more interest to me and for this investigation are the other two groups, even though they are minorities: Jews on the one hand, Christians on the other, who accept and respect the original story, who can both hear its first-century postbiblical Jewish interpretation but who differ, as have their two communities since the first century of the Common Era, on its application. This difference was originally intrafamilial and has been explicitly so described recently:[1] two groups of Jews, both of whom said, "That story is ours and applies to us. We are Isaac, in some sense, and certainly Isaac's heirs and beneficiaries."

One group are the Jews today who stand in the tradition of the Rabbinic heirs of the Pharisees and of the Sages before them. To this day, they understand and define themselves as Israel (the son of Isaac), as the people Israel, descendants, therefore, of Isaac and heirs of the benefits of his vicarious self-sacrifice ("the merits of the fathers"). This is not to say that these Jews always have Isaac's self-sacrifice in mind. Indeed, they do not often refer to it. It is to say, however, that, as Jon Levenson has argued, the stories of Isaac's self-sacrifice, the near loss and restoration of Rachel's children, and the paschal lamb of the Exodus undergird the heart of their identity as God's special people.

The other group are the Christians who stand in the tradition of those first-century Jews who believed in Jesus as the crucified and risen Christ. To this day, they identify Jesus as God's beloved Son, and they see and identify themselves as being, *in him*, heirs of God's

---

1. Alan F. Segal, *Rebecca's Children: Judaism and Christianity in the Roman World* (Cambridge: Harvard University Press, 1986).

promises to Abraham and his seed, and so the people of God. This *in him* was obviously of first importance to Gentiles who joined that Jewish sect, and for all Gentile Christians to this day, since they, unlike their Jewish coreligionists, had and have no other grounds for their claim.

That is not to say that this *in him* was not also essential for the Jewish members of the new movement. Their gospel, the one they formulated probably before any Gentiles had joined them, shows that Jesus had become for them the Isaac par excellence. They too, having their life from Christ's sacrifice, had their new existence *in him.* Indeed, their connection to Isaac in Jesus Christ may have been all the more vivid for them by being built upon their genealogical relationship to the patriarch.

The formation of the Christian movement, however, set the stage for rivalry, for there were now two groups, each claiming the same story and seeing itself as defined by that tale and heirs to its promises. They believed their claim to be justified for different reasons, of course. For the Jewish people, their ground was their physical descent from Abraham, to whom the blessings of Genesis 22:17-18 were promised by God. The ground for the Christians was their participation by faith and by the power of the Spirit in Jesus as the embodiment of Israel and the confirmation of all God's promises (Romans 15:8; 2 Corinthians 1:20). With tragic consequences for the future, each could and did come to denigrate the ground of the other's claim. Jews could and did say that the Christians' ground was merely spiritual or religious; Christians could and did say that the Jewish ground was merely physical. Thus an inevitable tension, potentially salutary, was transformed into cold hostility.

The rivalry between the two ultimately touches their understanding of God. God could surely not have two beloved sons, could he? Nor would it have helped had it been asked, "could she," for the stories of the expulsion of Ishmael (Genesis 21:9-21) and of Esau's loss of Isaac's blessing (Genesis 27:1-40) leave a hard impression, which was picked up in a late prophetic and again in an early

Christian writing: "I have loved Jacob, but I have hated Esau" (Malachi 1:2-3, my translation, cited in Romans 9:13). Was not the God of Israel a jealous god?

Rightly understood, God is indeed a jealous god according to Israel's scriptures, but this jealousy is precisely over Israel's undivided loyalty: "Hear, O Israel! *Hashem* ["The Name"] is our God, *Hashem alone.* You shall love *Hashem* your God with all your heart and with all your soul and with all your might" (Deuteronomy 6:4-5, my adaptation of JPS). The chosen servants of this god should be prepared to offer up to God that which is most precious to them, not because God needs any sacrifice, but because this god asks of his people their unreserved devotion. Rightly understood, the God of Israel is indeed a jealous god. But to think that God can love only one people and could not tolerate the service of more people than Israel is to stand the biblical witness to God's jealousy on its head.

Paul's quotation from Malachi can lead to a perverted conception of God's jealousy if we ignore that the prophet was not referring to Jacob and Esau but only using them typologically and polemically for their descendants: the people Israel stemming from Jacob, and the Edomites and Amalekites, Israel's enemies, stemming from Esau.[2] We are further misled if we fail to see that Paul cites Malachi in order to underscore the strangeness of what is surely central to the witness to God in Israel's scriptures: *Hashem,* the God of Israel, works out the divine purpose through particular individuals, lines of descent, and children. Particularity entails the choice of one rather than another: of Abram alone, of Isaac alone and Jacob alone, and not, in the last two cases, of their older brothers. Israel's scriptures, however, are misread if taken to be only about Israel. Their fundamental theme is Israel-among-the-nations, which is ultimately the theme of Israel-for-the-nations. Israel's calling, as the Jewish tradition has maintained, is for the sake of the whole of creation. It is

2. Brevard S. Childs, *Introduction to the Old Testament as Scripture* (Philadelphia: Fortress, 1979), 494.

false to the evidence to say that the Old Testament's theme is Israel-among-the-nations, whereas the New Testament's witness is to Israel-for-the nations. In both parts of the church's Bible, as in the Jewish tradition, Israel's existence, by its calling, is for the sake of the world — *tikkun olam* ("to mend the world").

The theme of divine choice of one-for-the-sake-of-all-the-others, central in the scriptures, can also be perverted if its second half is neglected. Both the Jewish and the Christian traditions did just that already in the first century of our common life together, each focusing on "the election of the one" (i.e., of themselves) and ignoring "for-the-sake-of-all-the-others," and that reading became fixed in both traditions. The sorry relationship between them over the centuries testifies to the cost of understanding election so self-centeredly.

Tradition, however, does not stand still and cannot, if it is the tradition of a living, developing community. What is handed on to us from the past comes with the unmistakable smudges of the fingers of our ancestors upon it, but it will not leave our hands to be given to the next generation without bearing our own dirty fingerprints, evidence of the history through which we shall have passed. After nineteen centuries of interpreting election as a matter of either/or, with unhappy consequences for both communities, some on both sides are finally trying to understand the other. Some on both sides are coming to see the inadequacy of thinking that the choice of one must entail the rejection of the other. That entailment is false to the biblical witness and false to the evidence of God's history with the Jewish people and the church. As Abraham was blessed in order to be a blessing for all the world (Genesis 12:2-3), so it has evidently pleased God to preserve and bless both God's people Israel and God's church in Jesus Christ. In order to bear witness to this further historical confirmation that the God of Israel is at the same time the Father of Jesus Christ, the quality of *either/or* ascribed to God's election should be tempered by the ascription of *this-in-addition-to-that*, or, even better, of *this-and-that-in-mutual-confirmation*.

It would be a serious mistake, however, to abandon the particularity of election, lest the originating identity of both communities be dissolved. According to the biblical story, the divine purpose is carried forward from generation to generation precisely by Isaac and by Rebecca, and just as specifically by Jacob and by Leah and Rachel, and then finally by Joseph and his brothers. It follows that it was carried forward by Sarah's son Isaac and not Ishmael, by Rebekah and not by any of "the daughters of the Canaanites" (Genesis 24:3), by Jacob and not Esau, and by Rachel, primarily, but also by Leah. The promises are passed along to Abraham's posterity by way of Isaac and Jacob and preserved for their heirs by Jacob's willingness to offer up his children by Rachel.

The particularity of God's election, therefore, defines the people Israel as God's "treasured possession among all the people" (Exodus 19:5), and their identity is marked by that intimacy rehearsed in the prophetic passages of Hosea and (Second) Isaiah:

> I fell in love with Israel
> > When he was still a child:
> And I have called [him] My son
> > Ever since Egypt. (Hosea 11:1, JPS)

> How can I give you up, O Ephraim!
> > How surrender you, O Israel?
> How can I make you like Admah,
> > Render you like Zeboiim?[3] (Hosea 11:8, JPS)

> But now thus says the LORD —
> > Who created you, O Jacob,
> Who formed you, O Israel:
> > Fear not, for I will redeem you;
> I have singled you out by name,
> > You are Mine. (Isaiah 43:1, JPS)

3. Admah and Zeboiim are the names of the two towns said to have been destroyed by God along with Sodom and Gomorrah (see Genesis 19), according to Deuteronomy 29:22 (in the Jewish Bible; 29:23 in the Christian Old Testament).

But hear, now, O Jacob My servant,
  Israel whom I have chosen!
Thus said the LORD, your Maker,
  Your Creator who has helped you since birth:
Fear not, My servant Jacob, Jeshurun[4] whom I have chosen,
Even as I pour out water on thirsty soil,
  And rain upon dry ground,
So will I pour out My spirit on your offspring,
  My blessing upon your posterity. (Isaiah 44:1-3, JPS)

Clearly, Israel cannot abandon the specificity of God's choice without dissolving the intimacy of its relationship with God.

No more could those Jews who discovered the gospel abandon their conviction of their election precisely in Jesus as God's beloved Son. The intimacy of their relationship with God, as well as of their successors in the faith, was grounded in their incorporation into Christ by the power of the Spirit, as they made clear, "called into the *koinonia* [communion, fellowship] of his Son, Jesus Christ our Lord" (1 Corinthians 1:9), in their being "the body of Christ and individually members of it" (1 Corinthians 12:27), "in Christ, a new creation" (2 Corinthians 5:17), branches drawing their life from Christ, who is the vine (John 15:5). "In him" (Ephesians 1:4, 7, 10, 11, 13), "in the Beloved" (1:6), is where they find themselves, because, they believe, that is where God has chosen to find them, and that is the grounds of their identity and their hope: "God is for us," because "he who did not spare his own Son but gave him up for us all, will he not also give us all things with him?" (Romans 8:31-32). Christian identity is and has been from the beginning identity in Jesus Christ, in God's Beloved Son, sacrificed and raised up "for us," the ultimate expression of the *aqedah* and so of the heritage of Abraham and of all the blessings he received. Clearly, Christians can abandon neither the specificity of the

---

4. Literally, "darling upright," a poetic appellation of the people Israel, according to Robert Young, *Young's Analytic Concordance to the Bible* (Nashville: Thomas Nelson, 1982), 541.

Father's relationship to his only begotten Son, nor their incorporation into him by the Spirit,[5] without dissolving their intimate relationship to God.

If the specificity of election is crucial to the identity of both the Jewish and the Christian communities, it can hardly be abandoned, but it could be modified without loss of its power. Indeed, if their continuing identity in the presence of each other is ascribed to God's providence and not to mere chance, then a modification of *either/or* by a *this-and-that-in-mutual-confirmation* becomes a theological necessity. The issue for both communities is whether their sense of intimacy with God can be tempered by their humility before the divine *pleroma* (fullness), so as to allow for an inclusiveness of divine love that rules out a "zero-sum" model for understanding God. Put differently, the issue is whether both communities can pay more than lip service to the strain within each tradition that insists that beside the great commandment to love God with all they are and have (Deuteronomy 6:5), there is another commandment that truly is like it: that they love their neighbor as themselves (Leviticus 19:18). The issue, at its most basic level, is whether both communities can be witnesses to a God who has preserved them both.

If this is to be, then they are going to have to learn to read their foundational stories in the scriptures with fresh eyes, and not only as some feminists have been urging for some time, but, in addition, with eyes open to the reality of two living communities of interpretation. They are going to have to learn a dual reading of their common scriptures. For one possible model on the Christian side, I close this chapter with a midrashic hymn or verse homily on the binding of Isaac from the Syriac Church of the fifth century.[6]

---

5. Incorporation into Christ was the very center around which John Calvin's theology turned. See Paul M. van Buren, *Christ in Our Place: The Substitutionary Character of Calvin's Doctrine of Reconciliation* (Edinburgh: Oliver & Boyd, 1957), esp. Part III.

6. This is the second of two fifth-century Syriac verse homilies, *Memra II*, ascribed to Mar Ephraim, published with notes, translation, and commentary by

It has the merit of supplying the missing voice of Sarah, so conspicuously absent in the biblical story of how her husband set out to slaughter her son. Sarah comes out as much or more "the knight of faith" than her husband in this reading, but I cite in part and in part summarize the text as an example of how a clearly Christian reading can leave ample space for a Jewish reading as well, and indeed has incorporated much from Jewish sources, as the notes will indicate.

(Ll. 2-5)	I begin[7] to lay before you/the story of holy people.
	Abraham, father of nations,/for one hundred years as though a single day
	Stood at God's gate/asking, amid groans
	and with supplication and prayer,/that he should have a son by Sarah.
(6-10)	This is granted.
(11-12)	Then God called out to Abraham: "Offer up to me your son as a whole offering/on one of the mountains I shall tell you of."
(13)	So Abraham begins to sharpen a knife.
(14-19)	Sarah sees this, and her heart groans. She asks Abraham to reveal what he is hiding from her, to which he replies that "this secret women cannot be aware of."
(20-32)	Sarah reminds him that they were as one in entertaining guests

---

Sebastian Brock, "Two Syriac Verse Homilies on the Binding of Isaac," *Le Muséon: Revue d'Études Orientales* 99 (1986): 61-129. I was led to this text originally by Burton L. Visotzky, *Reading the Book: Making the Bible a Timeless Text* (New York: Doubleday, 1991), 83-88. In the following partial citation, I follow the translator's line breaks, indicating the metric break of the Syriac.

7. Brock ("Two Syriac Verse Homilies") points out that the verb form could be used of both sexes but is more often used of a woman speaker or writer. This is his basis for suspecting that the author may have been a woman. The part Sarah plays in this text confirms that guess. The lines of the verse homily are given so that the proportion of space given to Sarah may be seen. Words in parentheses are those of the translator, supplied in order to convey the sense of the Syriac.

who turned out to be angels[8] and begs that she now be allowed to share with Abraham, whom she calls "drunk with the love of God," in the sacrifice of her only son.[9] Then to Isaac she says:

(33-38) "When you go with your father,/listen and do all he
            tells you
         . . . Stretch out your neck like a lamb./. . .
         lest his mind be upset/and there be a blemish in his
            offering."

  (39) "Listen . . . to the words of your mother/and let your repu-
         tation go forth unto generations to come."[10]
         Sarah lets them depart; they reach their destination and make
         ready to ascend the mount. As Isaac prepares to carry the
         wood,

  (47) a Voice says: "I shall put in him strength . . .

  (48) "and in this way shall I too carry/my cross in the streets of
         Sion,[11]

  (49) "When I go down to Golgatha/I will effect the salvation of
         Adam."

(50-56) So father and son begin to gather stones and build the pyre;

  (57) "They became workers for God,/the old man and his son,
         equally.

  (59) "The Threefold One blessed them/for they became (workers)
         for his Being."

(60-73) Isaac tells Abraham that he knows that he is about to be
         sacrificed and requests that he be bound tightly, lest he spoil

8. The reference is to the story in Genesis 18:1-15.

9. In this text, Isaac is more often called Sarah's only son, which in fact he is, than Abraham's.

10. The Christian author in no way reduces the significance of the sacrifice for Isaac's descendants, the future generations of the Jewish people.

11. The Christian typology is obvious, but Brock ("Two Syriac Verse Homilies") calls our attention to two midrashim in which Isaac carrying the wood for his sacrifice was seen by Jewish authors as the type for every Jew crucified by the Romans: *Genesis Rabbah* 56:3 and *Pesiqta Rabbati* 31:2.

the offering.[12] Abraham is much relieved to hear that Isaac is not praying to be spared what God has commanded.

(74-78) Abraham proceeds with the offering but is stopped by a Voice from on high that tells him:

(79) "Your offering is accepted . . .

(80) . . ./. . . become (father) to thousands without number."

(81) "And without mention of your name, Abraham,/an offering shall not be accepted."

(82) Abraham turns and finds a lamb "hanging on the tree,"[13] which

(83-98) he offers in place of Isaac. Upon their return home, Abraham tells Isaac to wait while he sees how Sarah will receive him. She welcomes Abraham, bringing water to wash his feet, and says:[14]

(99) "Welcome, blessed old man,/husband who has loved God;

(100) "Welcome, O happy one,/who has sacrificed my only child on the pyre;

(101) "Welcome, O slaughterer,/who did not spare the body of my only child."

(102-11) Sarah asks for a full report of how Isaac died and whether he wept, and Abraham assures her that Isaac did not. Sarah says:

(112) "May the soul of my only child be accepted,/for he hearkened to the words of his mother."

(113-24) Sarah grieves that she was not present and has not even seen the place where her only child, her beloved, was sacrificed.

(125-27) Suddenly, Isaac comes in. Sarah rejoices, saying:

(128) "Welcome, O dead one come to life."

---

12. The Palestinian Targum has Isaac asking Abraham to bind him securely so that the offering will be acceptable. The broader theme of Isaac's willingness for and cooperation in his sacrifice, which we saw in the postbiblical development of the *aqedah* sketched above in Chapter 4, is clear.
13. A bit of purely Christian typology.
14. Note the ascending bitterness of Sarah's welcome in the next three lines.

(129-38)   She asks Isaac, "What did your father do to you?" Upon hearing his report, she says:

(139)   "Henceforth, my son, it will not be 'Sarah's son'/that people will call you,

(140)   "but 'child of the pyre'/and 'offering which died and was resurrected.'

(141)   "And to You be the glory, O God,/for all passes away, but You endure."

CHAPTER 11

The Gospel in a Dual Reading of Scripture

In this penultimate chapter, I want to test the feasibility and possibilities of the dual reading of scripture proposed in Chapters 9 and 10, an interpretation that seeks to do justice to God's continuing history with the Jewish people as well as God's history with the Christian church. For this purpose I have selected three passages from three familiar family stories: Sarah's appeal to Abraham to expel Hagar and Ishmael (Genesis 21:9-13); Esau's discovery that he has been robbed of his blessing (Genesis 27:36-38); and, more briefly, the discussion, in a parable, between a father and his older son, on the occasion of the return of their lost son and brother (Luke 15:25-32). Each story is about parents and children, and it is not surprising that we come across difficult moments. The children's contribution to the difficulty varies from story to story, but the pain that we cannot but feel on reading each of the Genesis tales is aroused primarily by parental words or actions. The pain is only sharpened by the realization that according to these stories, God's intention or purpose is carried forward precisely by what pains us. In each of these stories, familial jealousy or sibling rivalry is central, and each has been used as a weapon, especially by Christians against Jews. They are therefore prime candidates for testing a dual reading, precisely because their traditional interpretation challenges the possibility of such a reading and of finding the gospel therein.

1

In the first story (Genesis 21:9-20), Sarah sees Ishmael "playing," a word with possibly negative connotations. William Tyndale caught this by translating "a-mocking"; Luther was also aware that the word might not be innocent and translated *"dass er ein Spotter war"* ("that he was a mocker"). Potiphar's wife uses the same word to accuse Joseph (Genesis 39:14), variously translated as "to mock," "insult," "do us shame," or "dally." In our first story, the Rabbis stretched it to mean "intending to murder"; perhaps they too felt that what Sarah is about to say needs some justification.

What Sarah says, in effect, is that Abraham should throw Ishmael and his mother Hagar out of the household. Sarah's explicit motive is jealousy, not for herself, but for her son Isaac as Abraham's sole heir. Abraham is unhappy about this request, but God tells him not to worry and to do as Sarah demands. He is told, in effect, that God's story will continue with Isaac but that God will make a nation of Ishmael too, for he is, after all, Abraham's son. So Ishmael and his mother are sent into the wilderness, but they are soon rescued by an angel who promises to make of the lad "a great nation."

So much for the story; now to our concern for a dual reading. Sarah is jealous for her only son, lest he have a rival for Abraham's heritage. As portrayed by the author, she is playing a "zero-sum game," as we say, a game in which one side's gain is automatically the other side's loss. There are such games, but the divine word to Abraham is that God does not play that way. The divine reply confirms that the story of Israel-among-and-for-the-nations will continue, and that Isaac will be its bearer.

Isaac's role as the sole bearer of this special story, however, entails his bearing it precisely for the sake of the nations of the world, of which Ishmael is explicitly promised to be a great one. Ishmael will therefore be a definite part of that story and one of its beneficiaries. If we keep in view the biblical focus on Israel's calling to be a holy nation — one nation singled out from, and for the sake of, all the others — we need not be upset by Sarah's jealousy, since God is able to use it, in spite of Sarah's intentions, in the service of that focus.

A dual reading challenges us to see that God's jealousy is not to be confused with human jealousy. God's jealousy, passion, zeal, (referred to explicitly in Exodus 20:5 and Deuteronomy 5:9, and in Exodus 34:14, for example) is for Israel's exclusive devotion, that it serve him alone as its God, and precisely for the sake of all God's creation. That is surely the thrust of the *aqedah,* and that was certainly emphasized in the saying of Jesus quoting the *Shema Israel* ("Hear, O Israel" — the central affirmation of Judaism), "You shall love *Hashem* your God" without reserve (Matthew 22:37; Deuteronomy 6:5). Human jealousy, on the other hand, although a powerful force to be reckoned with (as noted in Proverbs 6:34 and Song of Songs 8:6), favors some at the expense of others. Israel's scriptures hold up a contrasting behavioral example in Moses, who rejected the very thought of being jealous for his authority as God's prophet, with the words (Numbers 11:29) "Would that all *Hashem's* people were prophets!"

Before leaving our first story, a word should be said about Paul's much disputed use of it in Galatians 4:22-31. It is a matter of debate what Paul meant by calling his treatment of the story of Sarah and Hagar an "allegory" (v. 24), for in fact he lines up a series of terms in a relationship defined by the verb *systoichein,* "to correspond in pairs."[1] Each term is paired with its opposite, producing two columns:

1. For this reading of Galatians, and on the Pythagorean table of contraries as the key to Paul's midrash here, see Lloyd Gaston, *Paul and the Torah* (Vancouver: University of British Columbia Press, 1987), 83-91.

Hagar, slave	Sarah, free
Ishmael, born of the flesh	Isaac, born of promise
Sinai, a mountain in Arabia[2]	Present Jerusalem

On the traditional reading, when Paul says that Hagar (along with "Mount Sinai in Arabia") corresponds to the present Jerusalem, he intends all three to go in the same column. That puts "the present Jerusalem" in the "slave" column and leaves the "Jerusalem above" to be put in the "free" column. If the verb "corresponds" *(systoichein)* is to carry its usual rhetorical sense, however, the list should be as given above: "the present Jerusalem" goes in the *opposite* column from Hagar and "Sinai, a mountain in Arabia," and therefore in the same column as Sarah. This reading removes any anti-Israel implication from the passage, for Paul's "allegory," like his polemic, is directed not against Israel but against his opponents within the church.

It follows in either case that "the Jerusalem above," which is not listed as one of a corresponding pair, forms part of the conclusion. "Jerusalem above" is the city as it is promised to be, as we hear of it, for example, in Isaiah 54:11-14, with "all your gates of precious stones" (v. 13) and "safe from oppression" (v. 14). If it were placed anywhere, it would belong in the "Sarah" column, since it is "free" (v. 26).

The good news in a dual reading of this story is that we may drop the old idea that God's decision for Isaac entails the rejection of Ishmael. It makes visible what is clearly implied in *The Statement of Principles of Conservative Judaism,* that God's election of Israel is for the sake of all, that Israel is certainly God's beloved and precisely *for the good of the nations,* of which Ishmael is and will be a great

---

2. Following a well-attested variant reading, Gaston proposes that Paul knew the midrashic tradition that God offered the Torah to the seventy nations (and so from another "Sinai," "in Arabia"), each of which refused it, before offering it to Israel (Gaston, *Paul and the Torah,* 83-91).

one, and that therefore Ishmael will have a part in and be one of the beneficiaries of the story that Isaac will carry into the future.

2

The background to the second story (Genesis 27:36-38) is Isaac's preference for his son Esau, the all-around outdoorsman ("because he [Isaac] had a taste for game," Genesis 25:28), and Rebekah's preference for the homebody Jacob, by some seconds the younger of the twin brothers. One day, we are told, Esau comes home famished and begging for food, and Jacob demands Esau's birthright before letting him have bread and some of the lentil stew that he is cooking. Some while later, toward the end of Isaac's life, when he plans to give his final blessing to his older son, Rebekah, on her own initiative, maneuvers Jacob into Esau's stead, and she and Jacob (who cooperates fully) trick the old, blind Isaac into giving Jacob the blessing that he intends and is, as it were, saving up for Esau.

No sooner is the imposture accomplished than Esau comes in, discovers what has happened, and "burst[s] into wild and bitter sobbing" (JPS), or "crie[s] out greatly and bitterly beyond measure" (Tyndale), and says to Isaac, "Bless me, too, father!" Seeing that his father is either unwilling or unable to retract the blessing already given, Esau cries again, "Have you but one blessing, father? Bless me, too, father!" Then once again we are told, "And Esau wept aloud" ("lifted up his voice and wept" — Tyndale). Clearly, the author of this tale felt for Esau in his loss.

The presupposition on which the story depends is that a blessing, once given, cannot be retracted. Let us accept this and take the blessing as given. What Jacob wins by deceit, then, are four promises (Genesis 27:28-29): (1) economic, primarily agricultural, prosperity; (2) the service of peoples and the homage of nations; (3) lordship over his brothers, who will bow down to him; and (4) the promise that those who curse him will be cursed, and that those who bless him will be blessed. The first, second, and fourth parts of this fateful blessing are not small matters, but they need have caused no problem within the family. It was the third part of the blessing that cost Esau the most.

Irenaeus, a second-century bishop and theologian, noted the ironic aspect of the second and especially the third part of the blessing, pointing out that as the story unfolds, Jacob in fact served Laban fourteen years, and Jacob, on returning from that service, bowed down to Esau![3] We could even add that the painful third part of the blessing is only realized in Jacob's son, Joseph. This, however, does not take us to the heart of the matter, for Irenaeus' reading only throws doubt on Jacob's status, a move reflecting Christian hostility toward the Jewish people.

A dual reading, on the other hand, must raise a question about the nature of the promised lordship over one's brother. If it is modeled on God's lordship, then to be lord over one's brothers and worshiped by them is no denigration of them. If it is modeled on God's "almighty power," which is declared "chiefly in showing mercy and pity," to quote from an ancient prayer,[4] then Jacob is committed, by reason of the stolen blessing, to a more difficult task than Irenaeus ever imagined. Jacob, who will be renamed Israel, is thereby destined to be Israel-for-the-nations, for it is the will of Israel's God to be the Redeemer of all creation.

The problem in this story, then, does not stem from the blessing that Jacob/Israel received, for the blessing entails the assumption of an immense responsibility for his brothers. Rather, the problem is revealed in Esau's cry "Have you but one blessing,

---

3. Irenaeus, *Against Heresies* 5.33.3; translation available in Alexander Roberts and James Donaldson, eds., *The Ante-Nicene Fathers: Translations of the Writings of the Fathers down to A.D. 325,* vol. 1 (reprint; Grand Rapids: Eerdmans, 1973), 562.

4. Proper 21 in the Episcopal Book of Common Prayer, formerly the collect for the eleventh Sunday after Trinity, the 1662 translation of a sixth-century Gelasian collect. See Massey Hamilton Shepherd, *The Oxford American Prayer Book Commentary* (New York: Oxford University Press, 1950), 204-5.

father?" The problem lies in old Isaac's limitation. He was by then admittedly an old man — "old and his eyes were dim so that he could not see" (27:1) — but might he not have recalled for Esau the final clause of the blessing with which Jacob had been blessed? The last part of Jacob's blessing was "Blessed be everyone who blesses you."

For a later descendant of Jacob, the apostle Paul, that final blessing meant that Israel's calling was to be a messenger of hope for the nations, hope to which, as Paul himself could testify, the nations were responding positively. Paul saw this through his reading, in its Greek translation, of the tradition established by Jacob's descendants:

> As it is written, "Therefore I will praise you among the nations, and sing to your name" (Psalm 18:49 and 2 Samuel 22:50); and again it is said, "Rejoice, O nations, with his people" (a play on Deuteronomy 32:43); and again, "Praise the Lord, all nations, and let all the peoples praise him" (Psalm 117:1); and further Isaiah says (11:10), "The root of Jesse shall come, he who rises to rule the nations; in him shall the nations hope." (Romans 15:9-12, my translation)

Paul's may be a strong reading of Israel's tradition, but that does not make it a misreading.

If Isaac thought that he had only one blessing to give, the same cannot be said of Isaac's God, for God had a blessing for all future earthlings given to their original parents (Genesis 1:28 and 5:2). He also had a blessing for Noah and his sons, the new origin of humanity (Genesis 9:1). His blessing for Abraham also included the promise of a blessing for all who blessed him (Genesis 12:3), and although *Hashem* was "with Joseph," he also blessed Potiphar's affairs "for Joseph's sake" (Genesis 39:5). The God of Abraham, Isaac, and Jacob is a god rich in blessings.

However devious Jacob's manner of obtaining the blessing, no Christian should wish to question the story's message that he is the blessed one. God's promises and story were preserved by his descendants. The Jewish people are thus the children of the blessed Israel, and they are the ones to whom God has given his Torah. They are and remain to this day God's covenant partners, and so they are and will be until the day of their final redemption. To this day, they are called irrevocably to be God's Israel, called out from among and for the nations of the world. No Christian can wish to question any of this. Indeed, a dual reading demands that it be emphasized.

Then came Jesus Christ, born into and of Israel, called to relive its life as God's beloved Son, so that in him a community, drawn from all the nations, might live in Israel's calling and share his blessing. In him and in no other way, the members of this community inherit Jacob's blessing. They do so as Gentiles, not through the gift of Torah, and yet not without the knowledge of Torah, but with the full rights and responsibilities, in him, of sharing with Israel in the blessing of Isaac and the mercy of Isaac's God.

If Israel contests those rights, it does so largely because the church has refused for centuries to acknowledge the Jewish people as the Israel of God, and because it has tried to usurp their birthright and blessing. The church has acted in this way because it has not sufficiently believed its own gospel of the *crucified* Messiah. Jesus as the crucified Messiah, both is and is not Israel's Messiah. As the crucified Messiah, he brings God's power and promise to the Gentiles, but he does so by showing God's almighty power "chiefly in showing mercy and pity," showing himself in this weakness to be God's only begotten Son. As the crucified Messiah — that is, as the exhausted, bleeding, tortured, dead Messiah (for that, according to the gospel, is the one whom God exalted to his right hand on the third day) — he is anointed to just this humble task. In him, therefore, the church can only share in his weakness and humility, never able to boast of having done anything at all, much less of having displaced Israel. He is not that kind of Messiah, and that never was nor is his messianic task.

Jesus is therefore not the anointed heir of David whose coming will inaugurate or be the sign of a time of peace for Israel within history, in this world of time and space. The peace Jesus Christ left with his disciples was not that peace which the world (on occasion?) gives (John 14:27), but it is also not that peace for which Israel longs and hopes for "in the days of Messiah," namely, actual peace with its neighbors. A dual reading of the promises of God to Israel will never deny that most of Israel's hopes remain outstanding. The church will therefore join Israel in its hope for peace within this world, and also for the completion of the world's redemption by God, the resurrection of the dead, and the life of the world to come. It thereby confirms Israel's hope for redemption by the God of Abraham, Isaac, and Jacob.

3

We come, then, briefly, to our third family story (Luke 15:25-32), in which the father is the central figure, told not as a part of Israel's history, but as a parable by one who lived his life in the light of that history. The scene is set by the actions of the younger of two brothers, who insists that his father settle his whole estate on his sons, which he does: "he divided his living between them." Whereupon the younger son goes off and squanders his share. Reduced to ruin, he comes at last to his senses and returns home in the hope that his father will take him on as a hired hand. The father, however, takes him back as a beloved son and throws a party to celebrate his return. The older son, resenting this and refusing to join the party, is spoken to by his father: "Son, you are always with me, and all that is mine is yours. It was fitting to make merry, for this your brother was dead, and is alive; he was lost, and is found" (vv. 31-32).

Along with most interpreters, the last part of the story ignores a crucial line in the opening scene that must be stressed in a dual reading of it: "he divided his living between them."[5] Consequently, nothing remained to the father in his own name. He was a guest in his older son's house, and the party celebrating the younger son's return was entirely at the older brother's expense. The fatted calf on which all feasted, the best robe in which the younger son was attired — all were the property of the older son. Ought not the father, then, have asked his permission? In fact, he did not. Let us say that in his carefree joy over the return of his lost son, he forgot that all that remained of his living belonged, by his own act, to his older son. In any case, it is clear that the father does not play and does not even think of zero-sum games, and that he invites his faithful older son, and also the hearer of the story, to do likewise. He had already given away all that was his, so now, in effect, he can only invite us all to share whatever he has given to us with the least and the worst of our human family.

IN THESE REREADINGS of three family stories, we have changed nothing but only drawn out, in the first two, what is contextually important for the First Book of Moses yet insufficiently emphasized in the stories themselves, namely, that Israel, truly singled out and truly blessed, is chosen and blessed for the sake of the nations from among whom it has been selected. Jews as well as Christians know the importance of that context. It is beautifully expressed in Solomon's prayer of dedication of the Temple (1 Kings 8:23-53), which, as the Rabbis pointed out, makes clear that the Gentiles received more benefits from the Temple than did Israel.[6]

As for the third story, a dual reading only draws attention to a line hidden in its unfolding, which detracts in no way from the joy over the lost that was found. It also detracts in no way from the

5. The verse, as well as evidence for the law and for Jewish practice of the time, is thoroughly discussed by L. Schottroff, "Das Gleichniss vom verlorenen Sohn," *Zeitschrift für Theologie und Kirche* 68 (1971): 27-52, esp. 36-37, 39-42. See the literature cited there.

6. *Numbers Rabbah*, Bemidbar 1:3.

joy of all who have been so found, but it should remind them of the debt they owe to those who were always with the father, and to whom everything of the father's belongs. That is a fitting reminder for those whose good news centers in the death and resurrection of the beloved Son "according to the scriptures."

CHAPTER 12

Our Irreplaceable Old Testament

THE ARGUMENT OF THIS BOOK has been that the gospel that grounds the Christian church was produced by a distinctive reading of the scriptures of Second Temple Judaism, a reading that constituted the church's Old Testament. The chronological sequence of (1) the scriptures (in most cases, the Septuagint); (2) their postbiblical Jewish interpretation, including various messianic interpretations but also a retold *aqedah,* involving Isaac's self-sacrifice for the sake of his descendants, and his resurrection; (3) the early gospel as taught to Paul; and then (4) the various writings of the New Testament, is a sequence of literary dependence, each step of this sequence constituting a distinctive reading of the one that preceded it. The traditional view of the relationship between the Old Testament, as preparatory and preliminary, and the New, as definitive fulfillment, is therefore in need of serious revision.

The relationship between the Testaments will not be clarified by looking to that between the Jewish people and the church. The Jewish people and the church are both heirs of a common past. It would be absurd to say that of the two Testaments. The relationship will be more helpfully defined by reference to the history that we have examined in this study.

129

The chronological priority of the Old Testament is obvious: it came into being with the church itself. Further, the earliest Christian communities had no other sacred texts than those sacred to all other Jews. In time, a collection of the letters of Paul and others, and the Gospels and several other writings, were gradually added to the Greek translation of the Jewish scriptures as proper texts to be read when the church gathered for worship. When the additions had come to be accepted generally, then the distinction could be made between the original scriptures, the Old Testament, and the newer additions, the New Testament.

As we have argued, the original scriptures were sacred to the early Christian communities not just because the members of those communities were Jews. They were holy because they provided the language, images, and idiom with which those Jews learned to speak of Jesus as the rejected but then exalted Messiah (Psalm 89), as the Son of God (Psalm 2:7), as the Holy One of God (Psalm 16:10), and so of "Jesus Christ our Lord." They were the school books from which those Jews who were becoming the church learned to speak of Christ, the mine from which their gospel was quarried.

The implication is that those scriptures will remain sacred for a church that continues to read them as the source of its language and idiom for speaking of Christ and defining its gospel. They would lose that status for a church which found another source of language for speaking of Jesus and thus some other gospel than that which Paul learned and passed on. The continuity of the church today with that of the original gospel is dependent on the continuity in holding on to those scriptures.

As we have seen, the Jews who discovered the gospel read the scriptures figuratively or typologically, as many other Jews had been reading them for some time. They read them as having direct applicability to the present situation of their communities, and not merely as a document to be read in the past tense. We should not fault the authors of the New Testament, or the church fathers, for that matter, for having read the scriptures as being directly addressed to the church. How else is any community to read scriptures that it holds sacred? It holds them to be sacred just because it believes that in them it will find light and instruction in new situations. What we can and must object to, however, was the growing conviction of the church that those scriptures were originally, and so exclusively, addressed to them. In its place we have argued for a dual reading of those texts, a reading that reflects God's preservation of both the Jewish people and the Christian church as bearers of Israel's story into the future.

The church lived and thrived in its early years before it had a New Testament. It never existed without what it later came to call its Old Testament. This historical and substantive priority of the Old Testament, and the dependence of the New on the Old, should be reflected in the language the church uses to speak of the relationship of the Testaments to each other. For example, it is essential to the church's identity and the truthfulness of its account of its origins, that it acknowledge that the story of Jesus was certainly told, and may indeed actually have been lived, in such a way as to reflect or reenact the story of his people. When the church speaks in this way, it is stressing not only the solidarity of Jesus with his people and their history, but the fundamental continuity of God's work and presence in Jesus Christ with God's history with Israel. The church confesses this continuity whenever it speaks of and to the Father, Son, and Spirit as one God. Its Trinitarian confession affirms that the God at work as Spirit in the church is no other than the God of Israel who was present with his people and his world in Jesus. It was a serious distortion of this confession when the church began to say that Israel's story was essentially and originally (only) a foretelling of the story of Jesus. With this other claim, the church undercut the authentic novelty — not Marcion's total novelty, but novelty within continuity — of its own gospel and also tried to rob Israel of its story, turning its rites into what one English version of *Pange lingua* calls "types and shadows,"[1] as though types were only shadows and had no reality in their own right. The one confesses that God's work in Christ is a novelty within continuity and could lead the church to a healthy relationship of solidarity with the Jewish people. The other undercuts that novelty and also paves a road of contempt for Jews that others could — and did — extend until it led to Auschwitz.

In other words, the traditional Christian dispossessing reading, which forgets that it is one particular reading of Israel's scriptures, is unnecessary and actually weakens the element of novelty in the coming of Jesus Christ and so undercuts the witness of the New Testament. If the scriptures of Israel so simply foretell Christ, then the "discovery" of the gospel was merely a discovery of the obvious. But our investigation supports the witness of the New Testament itself that the gospel was a new word not previously heard, and one that gave the church both its Old Testament and then its New Testament. Both Testaments depended on that interpretation of Israel's tradition which produced that gospel.

This brings us, then, to one of the most interesting implications of our investigation, and that is the realization that to speak of "the christological interpretation of the Old Testament" is not only to speak tautologically; it is utterly anachronistic, implying that there was first an Old Testament, and then a christology derived from it (so a Christian might say) or read into it (as a Jew might say), and then used as a key to interpret those writings. The phrase and the idea it expresses ignore that it was in searching the scriptures in an attempt to understand the crucifixion of Jesus that the gospel was discovered. That discovery, however, was precisely the discovery both of christology, in its earliest form, and, at the same time, the discovery of the Old Testament. That is to say, it was a discovery of

---

1. Thomas Aquinas, the author of the hymn, was less crass; he called them *antiquum documentum*, "older patterns," which "gave way to the new rite" — *novo cedat ritui.*

the distinctively Christian way of speaking of Christ — according to the scriptures, and so, in the same act, a discovery of a distinctive reading of those scriptures which made them to be the church's Old Testament.

It follows from this, in my judgment, that the church should stand by and even rejoice in the name that it gave to its version of the collection of Israel's sacred writings: "the Old Testament." Arguments for replacing it with "the Scriptures"[2] or some other name, however well meant, ignore the story of how the church came to have its distinctive Old Testament. The overriding advantage of retaining the traditional title is that it is an implicit acknowledgment on the part of the church that this collection of writings is, for the church, inseparable from the interpretation it received in the church's coming to be, and that it has lived on in the church always through this interpretation. When we call it the Old Testament, we are acknowledging, even celebrating, the distinctive interpretation of Israel's scriptures from which the church lives.

A last but vital implication of this study, one so contrary to traditional interpretation, but one so forcibly implied by this study as to be unavoidable, is that the Old Testament is and ought to be the ultimate norm for the church's interpretation of its New Testament. The renewal or reconstruction of the church's relationship to the Jewish people has led to an awareness that there are a number of places in the New Testament that are so stained by the polemics of the first century as to raise questions about whether they should be read at all in the church today. Examples would be Matthew 27:25, where Matthew has "all the people" cry out, in response to Pilate's (historically utterly unlikely) protestation of Jesus' innocence, "His blood be upon be on us and on our children"; and John 8:44,

---

2. For one example of such an argument, see Paul M. van Buren, *A Theology of the Jewish-Christian Reality. Part 1: Discerning the Way* (New York: Seabury, 1981; reprint, Lanham, Md.: University Press of America, 1995), 122ff. An alternative suggestion is to call them "The First Testament."

the Evangelist's polemic against "the Jews," put in the mouth of Jesus: "You are of your father the devil, and your will is to do your father's desires." Are we to excise such passages from the New Testament, or ignore them, or just not use them? However that be decided, the prior question is, by what authority, according to what criterion, could any of these courses be chosen? This study has suggested an answer: by the authority of the Old Testament.

How or in what way can the Old Testament be used to censor the New Testament? As we have argued, the scriptures of Israel, read as the Old Testament, were the source book for the authors of the gospel and of the New Testament. The New Testament is therefore the copy book of the early church, a collection of first attempts to understand and interpret Jesus, his life and death, in accordance with the scriptures, which is to say, by the Old Testament. The Old Testament, consequently, is that to which the church should return again and again to review what the authors of the New Testament had to say about Jesus. If at times they forgot that they had only been able to understand Jesus as Israel's Messiah because he came clothed in Israel's scriptures, if at times they forgot that Jesus' story could only be told as Israel's story, and so set Jesus against his people or set their story at cross purposes with his, then at that point we need to listen with them to Israel's witness and not to their polemics. In this way, the Old Testament can help to protect the church from the polemical excesses of the first generation or two of those called to bear witness to Jesus Christ according to the scriptures. When we find them writing, for example, that Jesus' own people, the people Israel, said that they, not the Romans, were responsible for his death, then we have to go back to the Psalms, to the stories of Abraham and of David, to Isaiah 53. When we do so, we may discover that they have forgotten that, however much God's people have always been a problem for God, they have remained God's first love, and their story has been always our first and best guide to speaking of God's love for all God's creation.

However it be expressed liturgically and in the lectionary, there can be no question that the Old Testament is irreplaceable for the church. It remains what it was for the disciples of Jesus: the grounds for and the source of the actual vocabulary for telling the good news. For the church has no other news than the gospel "according to the scriptures." Tracing the discovery of that gospel and the consequences of that discovery has been our single quest in this investigation.

Works Cited

Barth, Karl. *Church Dogmatics.* 13 vols. Edited by G. W. Bromiley and T. F. Torrance. Edinburgh: T & T Clark, 1936-75.

Ben-Chorin, Schalom. *Bruder Jesus: Der Nazarener in jüdischer Sicht.* Munich: Paul List, 1967.

Borg, Marcus J. *Jesus in Contemporary Scholarship.* Valley Forge, Penn.: Trinity Press International, 1994.

Brock, Sebastian. "Two Syriac Verse Homilies on the Binding of Isaac." *Le Muséon: Revue d'Études Orientales* 99 (1986): 61-129.

Brockway, Allan, Rolf Rendtorff, Simon Schoon, and Paul van Buren. *The Teaching of the Churches and the Jewish People.* Geneva: World Council of Churches, 1988.

Brown, Raymond E. *The Death of the Messiah.* 2 vols. New York: Doubleday, 1994.

Carroll, John T., Joel B. Green, et al. *The Death of Jesus in Early Christianity.* Peabody, Mass.: Hendrickson, 1995.

Charlesworth, James H., ed. *The Messiah: Developments in Earliest Judaism and Christianity.* Minneapolis: Fortress, 1992.

———, ed. *The Old Testament Pseudepigrapha.* 2 vols. New York: Doubleday, 1983-85.

Childs, Brevard S. *Biblical Theology of the Old and New Testaments:*

Theological Reflection on the Christian Bible. Minneapolis: Fortress, 1993.

————. *Introduction to the Old Testament as Scripture.* Philadelphia: Fortress, 1979.

Collins, John J. *The Scepter and the Star: The Messiahs of the Dead Sea Scrolls and Other Ancient Literature.* New York: Doubleday, 1995.

Crossan, John Dominic. *Jesus: A Revolutionary Biography.* San Francisco: HarperSanFrancisco, 1994.

Dahl, Nils Alstrup. *Jesus the Christ: The Historical Origins of Christological Doctrine.* Edited by Donald H. Juel. Minneapolis: Fortress, 1991.

Dodd, C. H. *According to the Scriptures.* London: Nesbit, 1952.

Dunn, James D. G. *Christology in the Making: A New Testament Inquiry into the Origins of the Doctrine of the Incarnation.* 2d ed. Grand Rapids: Eerdmans, 1996.

————. *The Partings of the Ways between Christianity and Judaism and Their Significance for the Character of Christianity.* London: SCM; Philadelphia: Trinity Press International, 1991.

Emet ve Emunah: Statement of Principles of Conservative Judaism. New York: Jewish Theological Seminary of America, 1988.

Fitzmyer, Joseph A. *Romans: A New Translation with Introduction and Commentary.* Anchor Bible, vol. 33. New York: Doubleday, 1993.

Fredriksen, Paula. *From Jesus to Christ: The Origins of the New Testament Images of Jesus.* New Haven: Yale University Press, 1988.

Gager, John G. *The Origins of Anti-Semitism: Attitudes toward Judaism in Pagan and Christian Antiquity.* New York/Oxford: Oxford University Press, 1983.

Gaston, Lloyd. *Paul and the Torah.* Vancouver: University of British Columbia Press, 1987.

Hamilton, Neill Q. *Jesus for a No-God World.* Philadelphia: Westminster, 1969.

Hays, Richard B. *Echoes of Scripture in the Letters of Paul.* New Haven and London: Yale University Press, 1989.

Hengel, Martin. *The Pre-Christian Paul.* London: SCM Press; Philadelphia: Trinity Press International, 1991.

Hoffmann, R. Joseph. *Marcion: On the Restitution of Christianity.* Chico, Calif.: Scholars Press, 1984.

Hollander, John. *The Figure of Echo: A Mode of Allusion in Milton and After.* Berkeley: University of California Press, 1981.

Isaac, Jules. *The Teaching of Contempt: Christian Roots of Anti-Semitism.* New York: Holt, Rinehart, and Winston, 1964.

Juel, Donald. *A Master of Surprise: Mark Interpreted.* Minneapolis: Fortress, 1994.

————. *Messianic Exegesis: Christological Interpretation of the Old Testament in Early Christianity.* Philadelphia: Fortress, 1988.

Kähler, Martin. *Der sogenannte historische Jesus und der geschichtliche, biblische Christus.* Leipzig: Deichert, 1892.

Kee, Howard Clark. *Community of the New Age: Studies in Mark's Gospel.* Philadelphia: Westminster, 1977.

Kermode, Frank. *The Genesis of Secrecy: On the Interpretation of Narrative.* Cambridge: Harvard University Press, 1979.

Klappert, Berthold, et al., eds. *Jesusbekenntnis und Jesusnachfolge.* Munich: Kaiser, 1992.

Kugel, James L. "The Bible in the University." In *The Hebrew Bible and Its Interpreters,* edited by William H. Propp, Baruch Halpern, and David Noel Freedman, 143-65. Winona Lake, Ind.: Eisenbrauns, 1990.

————. "Two Introductions to Midrash." In *Midrash and Literature,* edited by Geoffrey H. Hartman and Sanford Budick. New Haven: Yale University Press, 1986.

Lapide, Pinchas. *The Resurrection of Jesus: A Jewish Perspective.* Minneapolis: Augsburg, 1983.

Lauterbach, Jacob Z., ed. and trans. *Mekilta de-Rabbi Ishmael: A Critical Edition.* 3 vols. Philadelphia: Jewish Publication Society, 1973.

Levenson, Jon D. *The Death and Resurrection of the Beloved Son: The Transformation of Child Sacrifice in Judaism and Christianity.* New Haven and London: Yale University Press, 1993.

Lightfoot, J. B. *St. Paul's Epistle to the Philippians.* London: Macmillan, 1890.

Mack, Burton L. *A Myth of Innocence: Mark and Christian Origins.* Philadelphia: Fortress, 1988.

Marquardt, Friedrich-Wilhelm. *Das christliche Bekenntnis zu Jesus, dem Juden.* 2 vols. Munich: Kaiser, 1990-91.

———. *Von Elend und Heimsuchung zur Dogmatik: Prolegomena zur Dogmatik.* Munich: Kaiser, 1988.

Moore, George Foot. *Judaism in the First Centuries of the Christian Era: The Age of the Tannaim.* 3 vols. Cambridge: Harvard University Press, 1927-30. Reprint, New York: Schocken, 1971.

Müller, Klaus. *Tora für die Völker: Die noachidischen Gebote und Ansätze zu ihrer Rezeption im Christentum.* Berlin: Institut Kirche und Judentum, 1994.

Neusner, Jacob. *Genesis Rabbah: The Judaic Commentary to the Book of Genesis: A New American Translation.* Atlanta: Scholars Press, 1985.

———. *Messiah in Context: Israel's History and Destiny in Formative Judaism.* Philadelphia: Fortress, 1984.

Neusner, Jacob, William S. Green, and Ernest Frerichs, eds. *Judaisms and Their Messiahs at the Turn of the Christian Era.* Cambridge: Cambridge University Press, 1987.

Nicholls, William. *Christian Antisemitism: A History of Hate.* Northvale, N.J.: Jason Aronson, 1993.

Pelikan, Jaroslav. *The Emergence of the Catholic Tradition (100-600).* The Christian Tradition, vol. 1. Chicago: University of Chicago Press, 1971.

Richardson, Cyril C., trans. and ed. *Early Christian Fathers.* Library of Christian Classics, vol. 1. Philadelphia: Westminster, 1953.

Roberts, Alexander, and James Donaldson, eds. *The Ante-Nicene Fathers: Translations of the Writings of the Fathers down to A.D. 325.* 10 vols. Reprint, Grand Rapids: Eerdmans, 1971-86.

Robinson, James M., and Helmut Köster. *Trajectories through Early Christianity.* Philadelphia: Fortress, 1971.

Samuel, Maurice. *The Gentleman and the Jew: Twenty-five Centuries of Conflict in Manners and Morals.* New York: Behrman House, 1977.

Sanders, E. P. *Jesus and Judaism*. Philadelphia: Fortress, 1985.

Schottroff, L. "Das Gleichniss vom verlorenen Sohn." *Zeitschrift für Theologie und Kirche* 68 (1971): 27-52.

Segal, Alan F. *Paul the Convert: The Apostolate and Apostasy of Saul the Pharisee*. New Haven and London: Yale University Press, 1990.

————. *Rebecca's Children: Judaism and Christianity in the Roman World*. Cambridge: Harvard University Press, 1986.

Shepherd, Massey Hamilton. *The Oxford American Prayer Book Commentary*. New York: Oxford University Press, 1950.

Silbermann, A. M. *Chumash with Rashi's Commentary*. 5 vols. Jerusalem: Silbermann Family, 1934.

Soulen, R. Kendall. *The God of Israel and Christian Theology*. Minneapolis: Fortress, 1996.

Spiegel, Shalom. *The Last Trial: On the Legends and Lore of the Command to Abraham to Offer Isaac as a Sacrifice: The Akedah*. New York: Behrman House, 1967.

Stendahl, Krister. *Paul Among Jews and Gentiles and Other Essays*. Philadelphia: Fortress, 1976.

Swetnam, James. *Jesus and Isaac: A Study of the Epistle to the Hebrews in the Light of the Aqedah*. Rome: Pontifical Biblical Institute, 1981.

Tanakh. The Holy Scriptures: The New JPS Translation according to the Traditional Hebrew Text. Philadelphia: Jewish Publication Society, 1985.

Twersky, Isadore. *Introduction to the Code of Maimonides*. Yale Judaica Series, vol. 22. New Haven: Yale University Press, 1980.

Tyndale's Old Testament: Being the Pentateuch of 1530, Joshua to 2 Chronicles of 1537, and Jonah. Translated by William Tyndale. In a Modern Spelling Edition and with an Introduction by David Daniell. New Haven: Yale University Press, 1992.

van Buren, Paul M. *Christ in Our Place: The Substitutionary Character of Calvin's Doctrine of Reconciliation*. Edinburgh: Oliver & Boyd, 1957.

————. "On Reading Someone Else's Mail: The Church and Israel's

Scriptures." In *Die Hebräische Bibel und ihre zweifache Nachgeschichte: Festschrift für Rolf Rendtorff zum 65. Geburtstag,* edited by Erhard Blum, Christian Macholz, and Ekkehard W. Stegemann, 595-606. Neukirchen-Vluyn: Neukirchener Verlag, 1990.

————. *A Theology of the Jewish-Christian Reality. Part 1: Discerning the Way.* New York: Seabury, 1981. *Part 2: A Christian Theology of the People Israel.* New York: Seabury, 1983. *Part 3: Christ in Context.* San Francisco: Harper, 1988. Reprint of all three parts, Lanham, Md.: University Press of America, 1995.

VanderKam, James C. *The Dead Sea Scrolls Today.* Grand Rapids: Eerdmans, 1994.

Vermes, Geza. *Jesus the Jew: A Historian's Reading of the Gospels.* Philadelphia: Fortress, 1981.

————. *Scripture and Tradition in Judaism.* Leiden: Brill, 1961.

Visotzky, Burton L. *Reading the Book: Making the Bible a Timeless Text.* New York: Doubleday, 1991.

Williamson, Clark M. *A Guest in the House of Israel: Post-Holocaust Church Theology.* Louisville, Ky.: Westminster John Knox, 1993.

Wills, Gary. *Lincoln at Gettysburg: The Words That Remade America.* New York: Simon & Schuster, 1992.

Wright, N. T. *The New Testament and the People of God.* Minneapolis: Fortress, 1992.

Young, Frances M. *Sacrifice and the Death of Christ.* Philadelphia: Westminster, 1975.

Index of Names

Index of Scripture References